MW00989715

How you communicate is how you connect.

Are you a...

MOTIVATOR
CHALLENGER
COMMANDER
HEALER
PROFESSOR
SEER
MAVEN

Frequencies are the hidden language of human connection.

Erwin Raphael McManus is a world-renowned speaker and author who has spent over 45 years studying human behavior and the art of communication. He has spoken to millions of people in over 100 countries.

Through his vast personal experience and exploration, he distilled human communication into a system of seven unique frequencies.

Understanding the seven frequencies will revolutionize the way you communicate with your audience, your employees, your teams, your family, and loved ones.

Are you ready to find your frequency?

BY ERWIN RAPHAEL MCMANUS

7

THE SEVEN FREQUENCIES OF COMMUNICATION

The Hidden Language of Human Connection

ERWIN RAPHAEL MCMANUS

Copyright © 2024 by Erwin Raphael McManus

All rights reserved.

Published in the United States
by The Arena Publishing
a division of The Arena Community, LLC.

Hardback ISBN 979-8-9910456-1-2
Ebook ISBN 979-8-9910456-2-9

Printed in the United States of America

www.erwinmcmanus.com

2 4 6 8 9 7 5 3

Second Edition

Book cover by Tess Roy

This book is dedicated to my son, friend, and business partner, Aaron Christopher McManus, and all the emerging voices who will lead us into the future.

CONTENTS

Contents

Contents

Words Are Magic

Words are magic. Words are as close to alchemy as we will ever come. Imagine for a moment that you could attain a superpower that allows you to leave your body and travel freely through time and space. Imagine if you could transcend beyond the limitations of your material being and rematerialize in the consciousness of another human being. This is exactly what words allow us to do.

My words are infused with my thoughts and ideas, my passions and desires; even my soul. Words travel beyond my flesh and bone and journey comfortably through the space between us. They carry the force and power of meaning and explode inside the consciousness of another human being like an atomic reaction. Words form sentences. Sentences form paragraphs. Paragraphs form chapters. Chapters form stories. Stories form humans.

Words allow us to touch without contact. They have the power to move masses without physical coercion or force. Words not only carry emotions but ignite them as well. It would not be an overstatement to say that words have the power to create and to destroy. They carry within them our hopes and dreams, our ideas and ideals, our fears and doubts. Words carry our past and our future. They are the material of every great love story. They form the story from which we come to understand ourselves.

Some of us are old enough to remember the old adage, "Sticks and stones may break my bones, but words can never hurt me." Even as children, we knew this wasn't true. A broken bone heals. Words, on the other hand, can leave permanent damage. Words—or more specifically, the words we speak—are our greatest source of power. Sticks and stones pale in comparison to the power of criticism or encouragement.

THE POWER TO CREATE

"Abracadabra" is the incantation spoken by the magician when he seeks to change reality. Its earliest recorded use was by the Roman savant Quintus Serenus Sammonicus in the 2nd century. He was known for his passion for language. We were told that his personal library consisted of about 60,000 volumes. He believed the phrase 'abracadabra' had medicinal powers. He was both a polymath and a physician who strangely brought magic and medicine together. It would be easy to dismiss his work as magical and not medical. After all, he believed that a phrase spoken over a human being could protect them from sickness and restore them to health.

Although the origin of the word 'abracadabra' remains unknown, there are several folk etymologies associated with the phrase and its beginning. The phrase 'abracadabra' has an uncanny similarity with the Hebrew phrase 'ebra k'dabri' which translates, "I will create as I speak." The similarity can also be seen in the Aramaic phrase 'avra kehdabra' which translates, "I create like the word."

Regardless of the etymology of this magical incantation, there may be no culture more profoundly shaped by this belief than Judaism. The power of this belief, "I will create as I speak," is clearly embedded in the culture of the ancient Hebrews. Six hundred years before the birth of Christ, the book of Genesis establishes the cultural psyche and beliefs of the Hebrew People. The opening chapter of Genesis establishes the framework for all that has come into existence.

The recurring statement in the first chapter of Genesis is built around three words: "And God said..." Everything that exists comes out of what is spoken. The words spoken create the reality to come. To believe in the God of the Hebrews is to believe that He spoke all things into existence. It is to believe that you have been created in the image of God. He has endowed you with this very creative power. By virtue of your nature, you too speak reality into existence. There is more to it than simply saying, "Abracadabra." Still, the person who masters their words carries within them the power to create what exists only in their imagination.

FIND YOUR VOICE

Believing in the power of the ancient phrase 'abracadabra' may be too great of an intellectual leap but there are phrases you have already discovered have more power than one could imagine:

I love you.
You matter.
You can do this.
I believe in you.

If these phrases can be described as a blessing, there are also those that are nothing less than a curse:

No one will ever love you.
You will never amount to anything.
You are worthless.
You are a failure.

There isn't a single one of us that has escaped the power of the words spoken into our lives. If words do not have a magical power, they certainly have a metaphysical power. Within our words, we hold the power of life and death. The first words spoken in the book of Genesis are, "Let there be light." We, too, seem to have the power to create darkness or light. If not in the world around us, certainly in the world within us. It may not be an overstatement to say that we are the sum total of the words that have been spoken into us, and that we have allowed to define us.

If 'abracadabra' sounds like gibberish to you, it might be good to remember that all words are sounds to which we attribute meaning. Language is a waterfall of sensory experiences that translate not only meaning but emotion and essence. "I love you," perhaps the most powerful three-word construct in the human language, has no meaning when it carries no emotion and does not come from a person's essence.

Sounds create words. Words create meaning. Meaning creates communication. Communication creates connection. Connection creates community. Community creates humanity. Humanity creates the future. The future begins with a sound.

We find echoes of this in Frank Herbert's epic tale *Dune*, written in 1965 but thrust back into the social consciousness in the recent films directed by Denis Villeneuve. In Herbert's story, there is one caste of people known as the Bene Gesserit. They carried a messianic prophecy and were known for their clairvoyant powers. They wielded a power known as "the Voice" that enslaved others to their commands. The unique powers that the young savior Paul Atreides had within him would only emerge when he found his voice. His journey was his ability to master "the Voice." If you can find your voice, you will find your power.

WORDS CHANGE US

In 2004, a book titled *The Hidden Messages in Water* became a New York Times Bestseller. It was written by a Japanese entrepreneur and pseudoscientist named Masaru Emoto. Emoto claimed that he had scientific proof that the crystallization of water physically changed based on what was spoken into the water. He provided endless photographs depicting the phenomenon of unique water crystallizations formed by the words that were spoken.

The theory was that words of affirmation created beautiful crystallization. Words that were demeaning and negative created deformed and unappealing patterns of crystallization. He also described a more specific experiment speaking into jars of rice. He claimed that when rice was spoken words of affirmation it fermented. When rice was spoken words that were demeaning, using dismissive language, the rice would then become rotten.

I remember very distinctly attending a TED Conference for the first time over twenty years ago. I met someone who had launched a bottled water company where every single bottle of water was spoken into with love and affirmation. I must admit I thought the concept was bizarre. I now wonder if this company was directly founded in response to the work of Masaru Emoto.

I don't know if speaking affirmations makes the crystallization of water more beautiful; I do know it materializes a beautiful effect on the human spirit. I don't know if telling a bowl of rice that it is a fool will cause it to spoil. I do know that if you tell a child they are worthless it will eat them alive inside. Whether our words can change water has virtually no significance to the social landscape of the human story. If our words change us, this changes everything.

THE STORIES WE TELL OURSELVES

It is not humans' singular ability to communicate that makes us unique. In fact, it is quite the opposite. Every species has a unique ability to communicate with one another. What separates humans is the complexity of our communication. This is where the art of communication is a profoundly human experience. Human communication goes far beyond the utilitarian need to transfer information. We are the species from which poets have emerged. It is not enough for us to share our ideas. We must share our souls. We are the species of nuance and humor and satire and sarcasm and deception. Language is our vehicle. Communication is our oxygen.

I do not think that it is incidental that the etymology for the word communication is the same as it is for that of community and communion. When communication connects deeply, we create community. When communication moves to the deepest levels of intimacy, we create communion.

Storytellers have always shaped our view of reality. It is in the stories we tell each other that we come to know who we are both as individuals and as a tribe. It is in the stories we tell ourselves that we find our identity most powerfully and profoundly embedded within us. History is not remembered by reality. History is remembered by story. You do not even know yourself apart from the story you believe about who you are.

Without trying to do an autopsy on a living being, our inherent need for story may be rooted in our neurology. Our brains seem incapable of storing an emotion without a story to carry it. This is why we often find it virtually impossible to extricate a negative emotion. We treat that emotion as if it is a singular isolated entity that exists within us. Emotions do not exist in a vacuum.

You cannot change an emotion if you do not change the story that gives it life. The story protects and sustains the emotion. The story ensures that the emotion remains a part of you. If you want to change an emotion, you must be willing to change the story. Who we are is embedded in the stories we tell ourselves. If we want to elevate our inner worlds we must elevate the story of us.

This is why the storyteller is the most powerful character in the human story. They tell us a story that we have not been able to tell ourselves. When a storyteller brings a message of hope it can lift us out of our despair. When a storyteller brings us a message of love they can save us from our own self-loathing.

When a storyteller brings to us a message of faith, we find the courage to rise above our own fears. Whoever tells the best story creates the future. All of this to say, the future belongs to the communicators.

A LONGING TO BE HEARD

There is a cautionary tale here that we should heed. The most powerful stories are the ones that pass the test of time. But like with most things in life there is an exception. A lie well told can have more power than a truth poorly expressed. If you are committed to speaking the truth, then you must be equally committed to speaking it powerfully. A message is at the mercy of the vehicle that communicates it to the world. If you carry within you a dream, a vision, an idea, or a future whose time has come, you must become a master storyteller.

A master storyteller is the person who has first themselves been consumed by the story they are telling. The master storyteller is simply sharing with you the story that has consumed them. The story is not simply something they share; the story is who they are at the very core of their being. The resonance of a master storyteller is authenticity. The nuance of that resonance is frequency.

My first encounter with communication frequencies had nothing to do with human communication, but with a whale. Somewhere deep within the waters of the North Pacific, a whale wandered alone. Oceanographer Bill Watkins first heard his strange voice calling in 1989 and his mystery whale song haunted marine researchers for years.

The typical Blue Whale has a call at a very low frequency between 10 to 40 Hertz, but the whale call Watkins recorded was pitched much higher.

After twelve years of observation, marine scientists at Woods Hole Oceanographic Institution were able to conclude that the idiosyncratic whale song was indeed coming from a single source. Not only was his call distinct, but his migration patterns also appeared to be unrelated to the presence or movements of other whale species. The whale's frequency of 52 Hertz became its name.

52 Hertz traveled across the Pacific Ocean searching for a mate or a pod but his search was unsuccessful. Even when this whale was within proximity of other whales, and well within hearing range, they remained deaf to him. They could not hear his call. Neither could he hear their call. No whale in the world spoke his frequency. Decades after his discovery he would be dubbed 'the loneliest whale in the world.'

When I first heard of 52 Hertz I instantly resonated with his story. I had come to realize that I naturally spoke at an alternative frequency to most of the world around me. My mission became to find those who hear at 52 Hertz and make sure they know they are not alone in the world.

UNLEASHING YOUR FREQUENCIES

Human communication at its core is about frequency. All of us speak at a unique frequency. We are all designed for not only communication but connection. Without communication, the connection cannot be made. People have an intrinsic need to be heard and understood. Communication is what connects the loneliest of us back into community. No one should travel through life alone.

Even when we are in proximity to one another, if we are speaking at the wrong frequency we will not be able to hear each other. I'm absolutely convinced that much of the breakdown in human communication is our belief that everyone should be on our frequency. The key to powerful communication is making the commitment and learning the skills to get on the same frequency as the person you want to reach.

This book is written for those who understand the critical importance of communication with the intention of helping each of us gain mastery of our unique frequencies. We are responsible for the frequencies we choose when we communicate. Everyone deserves to hear the most important messages of their lives in a frequency that resonates with them.

In the following chapters, we will unlock the seven frequencies of communication. We will break down each communication frequency, their uniqueness, and their power. Because communication is inherent to our humanity these frequencies are not static but dynamic. The goal of this process is to elevate your communication effectiveness by first identifying your core frequency and then expanding your capacity to access other frequencies.

QUANTUM ENTANGLEMENT

Recently I've been fascinated by quantum entanglement. Quantum entanglement is a phenomenon that occurs when a series of particles are generated, interact, or share spatial proximity in such a way that the quantum state of each particle of the group cannot be described independently of the state of the other. To put it simply, once two separate particles have interacted they are forever connected and affected by each other. On a human level, this would explain why an experience from twenty-five years ago still has a present effect on you today. From a scientific perspective, or at least from the world of quantum mechanics, there has been an entanglement with the particles that are you and the particles of the person you encountered decades ago. This entanglement is what we would call our relationships, our experiences, our memories, and maybe even our wounds. We are all entangled with each other. We are all a part of this intricate web we create through the words we speak.

This is why words have power. Words have a quantum effect. Words can inspire us. Words can elevate us. Words can change our perception of ourselves. Words can change our beliefs. Words can change our dreams. Words can shape our character. Words can change our lives. Words can change the world. Words can create the future.

Words are magic. *Abracadabra.*

Introducing the Seven Frequencies

I have been married to the same person for over forty years. Kim and I met when we were both twenty-two years old getting our master's degrees. We were from different worlds with very little in common. She is a country girl from the mountains of North Carolina raised by a foster family on a farm. I am a first-generation immigrant from El Salvador who grew up in three major cities: San Salvador, New York City, and Miami.

We saw the world through divergent lenses. Our life experiences were almost in complete contrast to each other. We were aliens from different planets having to learn each other's language. When you are young and you fall in love you do not think about compatibility. A year into our marriage, we began to experience the reality that we were naturally and almost always on different wavelengths. Fortunately, we both found the other valuable enough to learn how to get on each other's wavelength.

Without communication our marriage would not have lasted. I have fallen in love with Kim a thousand times over since the first time we met. Every time we have a communication breakthrough we have a stronger marriage and a more wonderful romance. Communication is the most intimate act between two human beings. Communication is the singular competency that transcends into every arena of human development. Whether you are trying to connect with one person or millions, your ability to communicate will determine your ceiling. The key is getting on the same wavelength. This principle applies to our children as well.

I work with both my kids in different capacities. My son Aaron is in his mid-thirties and is the host of the *Mind Shift* podcast as well as the founder of The Arena Mastermind and conference that coaches entrepreneurs, creatives, and content creators across the world. He is also the creative director of our fashion brand Ghost Artifacts. We work together in the areas of personal and corporate coaching.

My daughter Mariah is in her early thirties and she began songwriting when she was twelve years old. She is now a recording artist under the name Riah. Through Mosaic, our community of faith, she created a global music movement called MSC. MSC signed with a major record label and their music has been listened to by tens of millions of people across the world.

Their success is something I am very proud of but that is not why I mention them here. I mention them because they both have chosen to purchase homes within ten minutes of me and Kim to stay close as we do life together. Perhaps the greatest achievement of my life is that my adult children are my best friends. We, of course, have our struggles and our conflicts. The key to raising children who become your closest friends is communication. Learning how to listen and how to be heard is everything. If your kids do not feel understood they will drift away. To be understood is to be seen. To be seen is to be valued. When you are heard you feel valued and loved. To foster life-long relationships with a person you love you have to get on their wavelength.

ON THE BIG STAGE

I begin here because when people ask me how I developed my ability to speak they are always focused on the massive platforms and big stages. Do not get me wrong. I love that my life journey has led me to speak to millions across the world. If I had not developed my ability to communicate I would have never traveled to nearly 100 countries and six out of seven continents. The stages I have spoken on have varied from 30,000 in South America to over 100,000 in Seoul, Korea, to an arena of 20,000 in Sydney, Australia and a stadium of 30,000 in London, England. Some of my favorite events have been in unexpected places such as Taipei, Taiwan, Kuala Lumpur, Malaysia, Hong Kong and Singapore. I am very much aware that developing my gifts and skills as a communicator has opened the world to me and allowed me to stand on some of the world's most influential stages.

Still, the art of communication is not all about getting on the big stage. More often it is about getting into the small rooms that are inaccessible without an invitation. Those rooms have set me on a more unexpected journey to the road less traveled. The key that opens those rooms is your ability to communicate at the highest level. The ability to connect to people from all over the world and from any facet of life has opened doors for me in unexpected countries like Syria, Pakistan, Cambodia, China, Turkey and

Cuba. One conversation I will never forget took me to Lebanon, where a door opened for me to meet with members of Hamas.

Yes, there are other factors that have made all this possible, but without the ability to communicate at the highest level none of this would have ever happened. Whether you want to save your marriage or scale your company, it all begins here. As we dive into an exploration of the seven frequencies of communication I hope we can get on the same wavelength.

RESONANCE

Historically, we humans have been mostly unaware of how frequencies impact our internal well-being. A more recognizable example of how frequencies impact us is through the effect of music. When you hear a particular frequency in music, it evokes a certain emotion. You find this connection between sound and emotion in experiences like worship or when you go to a concert. A ballad evokes the emotion of lost love. An anthem can make you feel as if you are ready to face your next battle. A serenade can make you feel more romantic. An orchestra performing Mozart can evoke an ecstatic experience of awe.

Frequencies go beyond music. When you are out in the woods and listening to the sound of running water, the calm frequency of nature creates a calm within your own soul. The intense frequency created in rush hour traffic when a hundred different sounds converge into noise can create anxiety, even anger within you.

No frequency compares in power to human communication. For many years I have studied how communication connects and disconnects. A frequency that draws the attention of one person may turn off the attention of another. To put it simply, a communication frequency is how we transmit our thoughts, feelings and essence through the spoken word.

Have you ever had a friend tell you, "You have to listen to this speaker, they changed my life. They will change your life." Then when you listen to the same speaker you feel no connection? Or maybe you heard someone share something that absolutely resonated with you. They were so compelling, so powerful, so life-changing, that you invited your friends to hear them but they did not have the same experience?

How a communicator shares their message determines its resonance as much as the words they speak. Their message will be more readily embraced and received by us if their frequency resonates with us. If their frequency does not connect with us, their message will not be accepted. Even if the message is true. Even if the message is important. Even if the message is essential for our lives. The frequency must connect for the message to take hold.

THE SEVEN FREQUENCIES

Together we are going to unwrap the seven frequencies of communication. Here we will elevate the hidden language of human connection. We humans are complex creatures who are dynamic and not static. We must never limit the unique capacity for humans to grow and develop. No system or framework can fully capture all of who we are as a species. We are all more than any description of us.

Understanding this, we also know that we do have dominant patterns and wavelengths that explain us well and that can bring us tremendous insight for personal growth. What I have distilled after forty-five years of studying human behavior and communication patterns has resulted in a system of seven signature human frequencies. We will go into depth on each frequency in the chapters to come.

Let me now introduce you to each frequency with a brief description. I feel certain you will recognize most if not all of them:

FREQUENCY #1: *The Motivator*
The Motivator frequency transmits energy and infuses self-belief.

FREQUENCY #2: *The Challenger*
The Challenger frequency transmits courage and awakens calling.

FREQUENCY #3: *The Commander*
The Commander frequency transmits trust and provides direction.

FREQUENCY #4: *The Healer*
The Healer frequency transmits acceptance and extends wholeness.

FREQUENCY #5: *The Professor*
The Professor frequency transmits knowledge and assures competency.

FREQUENCY #6: *The Seer*
The Seer frequency transmits vision and generates innovation.

FREQUENCY #7: *The Maven*

The Maven frequency transmits a new reality and creates paradigm shifts.

By the end of this book you will have begun your journey to:

- understand the seven different communication frequencies
- identify your core communication frequency
- discover which frequencies naturally resonate with your core essence
- unlock the frequencies essential to making your particular message resonate with your audience

CORE FREQUENCY

Each of us has a core frequency that serves as the foundation of our communication. It can also be described as your primary frequency. We will use both words throughout the book. Your core or primary frequency is the frequency that you use the most and expresses your most authentic self. It is the frequency you use when you do not know you are using a frequency.

Great communicators develop multiple dynamic frequencies that they access freely and easily. Many leaders who communicate often to their teams or colleagues will find they have developed a frequency cluster of two or three uniquely different frequencies working together. It is crucial to recognize which frequencies are most innate to you and which ones you might need to develop further.

I am absolutely confident that you have at least one dominant communication frequency and that this singular frequency is your core and primary voice.

UNLOCK YOUR FREQUENCY

If you would like to engage the material ahead with the benefit of knowing your core frequency let me encourage you to pause right now and go to www.thesevenfrequencies.com to take the seven frequencies assessment. It will be forever true that self-awareness is the beginning of personal growth and leadership development.

THE BUILDING IS ON FIRE

We all want to connect with someone. More than that, we all need to connect with someone. We all have a message we need to communicate. In one moment, your message could be as straightforward as, "Evacuate now, the building is on fire." In another moment, your message could be as complex as, "We have to let you go from the company," or, "I think we should just be friends."

Your message will use your frequency to connect to your listener. You must determine which frequency will best serve your message so you can best serve your listener. Effective communication often requires a blend of multiple frequencies. Understanding and accessing these frequencies can enhance our ability to connect with others and lead effectively. You can adapt to different situations and audiences by cultivating an awareness of your own strengths and areas for growth. The flexibility to move between frequencies not only enhances communication but also builds trust and confidence with your listener.

COMMUNICATING IS LEADING

The seven frequencies often operate in alignment with each other. The frequencies complement one another in unique ways. Your frequency is not meant to be a static version of you. You are more than a frequency. You may be trapped in a frequency and all the others are dormant. I can assure you that at least two or three other frequencies are waiting in the wings for you to call them up.

Communicating is leading. When you lead, you create a unique environment and culture. As you engage with the seven frequencies, imagine different scenarios you frequently face that could be better served by one frequency or another.

I hope you will get to the place where you have every frequency you need accessible to you. You can read your audience and know what frequencies they need so they can connect most powerfully to the ideas, vision, or truth that will change their life.

AN ART AND A SCIENCE

The beauty of the seven frequencies is that they are a human experience that permeate every aspect of our lives. They are not something we take on or do; they are an extension of who we are as unique individuals. This means the application for the seven frequencies is as vast and varied as the human experience. Understanding the frequencies will change the way you talk to your spouse and to your children, not to mention how you listen. It will change the way you communicate with your teams and with your friends. It will change the way you talk behind closed doors and how you speak on the biggest stages. The greatest communicators in the world understand that communication is both an art and a science. If you are committed to making the deepest human connections possible, then let's begin the journey to discover the hidden language of human connection.

MOTIVATOR

THEMES
Encourager | Enthusiast | Inspirer

FOLLOWERS
People listen because you make them feel
good about life and themselves.

POINT OF VIEW
"People need me to lift them up."

DRIVE
"I must bring energy to the room!"

MARKER
Do others look to you for encouragement?

DYNAMIC
Relating

HIGH NEED
Self-Belief

BASIC NEED
Energy

ICON
Steve Ballmer

COLOR
Sunburst

CULTURE CREATED
Positive | Optimistic

www.thesevenfrequencies.com

Motivator

F*ive of us decided to swim from the shore to the small island, just barely within sight of the horizon.*

All of us were good swimmers in the prime of our youth. The water looked fairly calm from the shore and the swim easy enough. As we began to swim toward the island, the waters began to intensify and quickly became more challenging than expected.

We discovered Nathan was the weakest swimmer among us when he began to fall back and tire.

At first we were so focused on the island's beach that we were unaware he was fading and struggling to keep afloat.

Vivian, who we called Viv, was the best swimmer among us.

She noticed that Nathan began to labor and fade away from the group.

Viv fought her way back against the current until she reached him.

She did not try to save Nathan by turning him on his back and then towing him to shore.

She simply began to swim by his side, just slightly ahead of him. It was almost as if she were pulling him forward with the force of her strokes.

Sometimes she simply guided him with stroke-by-stroke encouragement.

"Left, right, left, right."

Other times she reminded him that he had more capacity than he knew.

Over and over again she told him, "You can do this."

"You've got this."

"You were built for this."

"Breathe! Stroke! Fight! You got this!"

She breathed encouragement and intensity into Nathan.

I do not know if he would have made it to the beach without her.

Viv was one of the most powerful examples of a Motivator I have ever seen.

EVERYONE NEEDS MOTIVATION

The Motivator is the first frequency of communication I want to introduce. I begin here because I am convinced Motivators are the most popular. We love Motivators because they are always for us. When a Motivator speaks, their frequency gets inside of us and elevates our self-belief. A Motivator helps us find energy and strength we did not know we had.

If Motivator is your core frequency, you are driven to encourage people. You have a deep sense of responsibility to elevate the level of energy, excitement, and culture of the room. People are drawn to Motivators because they make them feel optimistic about life and about themselves. The Motivator constantly lifts people up.

Oftentimes in great stories the sidekick carries the Motivator frequency. Think of Samwise Gamgee from *Lord of the Rings* or

Neil Fak from *The Bear*. For me, the most iconic Motivator in pop culture would be the character John Keating from *Dead Poets Society*. Keating, played by Robin Williams, was a teacher who dramatically altered the lives of his students by using poetry as a gateway to seize the day.

Growing up, I often struggled in school. I had a difficult time paying attention or being engaged with a subject I found unimportant. When I had a Motivator as a teacher, everything changed. Maybe you have experienced this. A Motivator can make you feel excited about any subject, even if it is not your domain of interest. Suddenly you realize you are not just in a math class; you are in a motivational living class. Motivators take any subject and turn it into an opportunity to change the way you engage with life.

I have been grateful throughout my life for the different Motivators I have known. One of my closest friends is Jon Gordon, who has written over thirty books and is one of the most popular speakers across America. His internationally best-selling book *The Energy Bus* is about utilizing the power of positive energy to transform your life. For me, he is the perfect depiction of a Motivator.

Another friend of mine who personifies the Motivator is Angela Davis. I met her when she was the elite celebrity trainer for SoulCycle. Angela is a world champion sprinter and lifelong athlete but her greatest talent is changing the energy in a room and calling people to believe they can do more.

We collaborated often. She would listen to my talks, capture a few thoughts, and use them in her classes. When I heard her share my thoughts through her gifts as a Motivator, I thought, "I know I said that, but not like that!" Angela's motivational energy transformed simple ideas into powerful calls to action.

Even though I did not have the physical capacity to survive an entire training session with her, I felt the power of her motivation. She would call out, "Give a little bit more! How are you going to step into this moment? How you do one thing is how you do everything. Come on! Turn up the intensity!"

THE TRANSFERENCE OF ENERGY

All frequencies speak into a basic human need and a high human need. The Motivator speaks into the basic need for energy. Humans need a higher level of energy to face life's greatest challenges. During the COVID-19 pandemic, many people lost their sense of motivation and energy. Lethargy and apathy became pervasive. I experienced this myself. Some days I just did not have the energy to face the challenges ahead. Years later it appears that one of the long-term consequences of the extended quarantine in cities like Los Angeles is a generation of young people who struggle to find the energy to face many of the challenges of everyday life. If you have ever felt this way, you need to get around someone with the Motivator frequency. When you are impacted by a Motivator, you feel the transference of energy from them to you.

The high need a Motivator meets is self-belief. When they speak somehow their self-belief becomes your self-belief. A Motivator uses their influence to transfer their conviction and energy into you.

If you carry the Motivator frequency you know what I am talking about. When you walk into a room, you are not your priority. Your mission is to elevate the room. You want to help every person find courage. Find strength. Find the will to face whatever challenges they encounter.

An icon like Steve Ballmer comes to mind when I think of Motivators. Ballmer, the owner of the Los Angeles Clippers basketball team, can always be found cheering on the sideline, clapping uncontrollably like a 12-year-old kid having the time of his life. He fills the room with his incredible enthusiasm and positivity. Despite years of underachievement from his team, Ballmer's infectious energy keeps fans and players optimistic and hopeful. Ballmer is not diminished by setbacks. He always believes their championship season is just around the corner.

POSITIVE ENERGY

The Motivator believes people always need to be encouraged. All you need to succeed is a better frame of mind. A positive mental attitude changes everything for the Motivator. Their mantra is, "If you believe it, you can achieve it." They see it as their responsibility to bring energy to the room.

When the Motivator is a communicator's singular frequency, it can leave the hearer frustrated when motivation is not enough. The Motivator's encouragement can begin to feel superficial and out of touch with reality. The Motivator may not realize that to acknowledge a problem is not the same as being negative.

When a Motivator finds themselves discouraged, they can move into a non-communicative mode. Even Motivators need to be motivated. Negative environments can be especially toxic to those whose primary frequency is the Motivator. For the Motivator, energy is a 360-degree experience. They bring energy to the room and need energy from the room.

THE CULTURE YOU CREATE

Every frequency creates a culture. The primary frequency in a home or workplace will shape how they operate. The Motivator creates a positive and optimistic culture. Not a culture that lives in denial, but one that believes in solutions. Motivators can often be dismissed as unrealistic. The truth is that they simply see problems clearly without being overwhelmed by them. They see potential in people, teams and communities to overcome any obstacle.

Another iconic expression of a Motivator would be Ted Lasso. Now, I know what some of you are thinking. Ted Lasso is not a real person. But my response is, or is he? *Ted Lasso* is one of my favorite series of all time. I love the dilemma of an American college football coach going to England to become a coach of a professional soccer team. He knows nothing about soccer, and he is brought there by the owner because they want the team to fail. The owner thinks because Ted Lasso knows nothing about the sport, he knows nothing about winning. It was a terrible mistake to make. We discover Ted Lasso is an intrinsic Motivator and that his frequency transcends both the sport and the culture.

Even though he does not know anything about the sport, he knows so much about people that he immediately understands what the team needs. First of all, they need a transference of energy. They are on a losing streak. They have a bad culture. They are depressed. They are discouraged. They do not have any level of self-belief, and so his theme is belief. He puts up a physical sign in the locker room that says 'Believe,' but the team is still in jeopardy every single match because they do not believe.

Ted continues to bring positive energy to his team and that transference of energy eventually begins to take hold and transforms the culture. Motivators understand that people need the energy to take on great challenges but, more than that, they need a foundation of self-belief. By the end of the show, 'Believe' is not just a sign on a door. It is tattooed, carved and branded into the hearts of every player.

CHALLENGER

THEMES
Persuader | Exhorter | Confronter

FOLLOWERS
People listen because you inspire them
to be more and do more.

POINT OF VIEW
"People need me to call out the best in them."

DRIVE
"I must raise the standard!"

MARKER
Do others look to you to call them to a higher standard?

DYNAMIC
Activating

HIGH NEED
Mandate

BASIC NEED
Courage

ICON
Pep Guardiola

COLOR
Crimson

CULTURE CREATED
Activist | Achiever

www.thesevenfrequencies.com

Challenger

We were up 32 to 7 at halftime. All the pundits of the game predicted it would be close and if either team was expected to win, it was not us. Vegas must have been in absolute chaos by the end of the second quarter.

It would be an understatement to say we were feeling pretty good about ourselves. We were dancing like the game was over and the final verdict in.

When Coach walked into the locker room we were expecting nothing less than adulation and praise. Looking back, I don't know why.

All Coach seemed to remember from the first half were the seven points we gave up and the one drive we did not score.

He began challenging us to strive for perfection. If we were already satisfied there was no reason to go back out on that field. Our apathy was the enemy.

The score did not matter. What mattered was our effort. His focus was all about whether we achieved our potential, whether we optimized our capacity, whether we took hold of every opportunity.

The other team was not the enemy. They were not our competition. They were irrelevant. The only thing that mattered was how we wanted to be remembered.

Coach reminded us that we were the material from which legends are made. In the second half we would choose our legend. Winning was not enough. He expected our best until the last second, until our last breath.

We left the locker room with an intensity that led us to crush our opponent. When the Challenger frequency gets into your system, you are fire and ice at the same time.

THE POTENTIAL FOR GREATNESS

The Challenger is a very intense frequency. The Challenger lives in a world full of possibilities and the possibilities are always for personal development. The Challenger sees where we could be doing better or doing more. They crave improvement. The Challenger sometimes feels incredible frustration that other people do not feel the same need to make things better. They can never leave things alone. They can never leave things as they are. They are unsatisfied with the status quo. They are allergic to mediocrity.

Ironically, many of the voices that we consider to be motivational speakers are, in actuality, Challengers. Some of the most popular Challengers in the world of social media are voices like David Goggins, Tim Grover, and Ben Newman.

If you are in a relationship with a Challenger, you have been given a great gift. They can see in you the potential for greatness, even when you do not.

THE PRESSURE COOKER

Wherever the Challenger communicates, they elevate the room. Often the Challenger will construct a crisis that creates a pressure cooker for change. They believe that the crucible is where you become the best version of yourself. For the Challenger there is no growth without suffering. Pain is the only proof of effort. The frequency of the Challenger can create an incredible, almost unbearable level of intensity. The Challenger will always look for the arena where you can develop and strengthen.

The Challenger sees their role in life as being a catalyst for improvement. Not just incremental improvement. They can ask for exponential, radical, intense, seemingly impossible improvement. Their belief transfers to the listener and people are inspired to be more and do more. The Challenger's perspective of their relationship to the world is that people need the Challenger to call out the best in them. Many Challengers believe this because of the people in their life who called the best out of them.

FACE THE CHALLENGE

It fascinates me to see Challengers in a room together. One of my friends that is listed among the top communicators in the world is Ben Newman. If you do not know Ben, imagine Thor and you will be close. Ben is one of the founding members of my McManus Mastermind. One night during a Mastermind session, I watched a room of a dozen high-octane, testosterone-filled, highly competitive men begin to challenge each other in the area of physical prowess.

Ben invited them all to work out with him the following morning. They had all been talking about their various workout routines and each one of them was more than impressive. As Ben began to describe his workout, a few of them tapped out right away.

Let me give you the breakdown:

- 4:44 reverse plank (laying on back, feet 6" off the ground)
- 4:44 plank straight
- 250 jumping jacks
- 250 air squats
- 4x44 calf raises
- 44 kettlebell curls
- 2x44 pushups straight
- 4x44 abs
- 4x44 sec. cardio burst
- 4x44 sec. wall sits

And then you finish with 500 pushups.

A few of the bravest heard this list and joined him anyway. He nearly killed several of the most fit men I have ever known. This was of great concern to me since he was reducing the number of men who could be in my Mastermind.

Ben is a Challenger. His Instagram handle is @continuedfight. If you ever take the time to listen to his messages on optimal performance, make sure that you buckle up first. If you need an image to understand the Challenger frequency, imagine having an unlimited supply of Red Bull inside of your soul that you are determined to share with the world.

If you do not know much about football, the Miami Dolphins are the only team in professional football that ever had a perfect season. In 1972, the Dolphins did not lose a single game and went undefeated, culminating in winning the Super Bowl. The year before their perfect season they also made it to the Super Bowl, but they lost. I remember years ago I was in a conversation with someone who played for the Miami Dolphins.

The player told me how their coach Don Shula came into the locker room after they lost the Super Bowl and told them he wanted them to remember that feeling. Shula used the moment after their most devastating defeat to prepare them for the greatest season of their lives and in pro football history.

This is the dynamic of the Challenger. They use every opportunity to call out the best in people. Whether it is a loss or a win, a failure or a success, the Challenger simply sees it as the material to get better.

THE COURAGEOUS SOLUTION

When you resonate with the Challenger you feel inspired to keep elevating and aspire for more. But let's be honest, we do not always feel like being challenged. A Challenger frequency when unmitigated can make you feel that you are never enough. Their continuous call for greatness can leave you exhausted and even create a sense of inadequacy. If your primary frequency is the Challenger, the person you hope to inspire might instead wonder, "Am I doing anything right? Are you ever going to affirm me? Are you ever going to acknowledge all that I have accomplished?"

A Challenger does not believe you need their affirmation as much as you need their drive. The audience is a room of coals and the Challenger brings the fire.

The Challenger sees the world as in need of courage. This is the basic need the Challenger tries to meet through communication. The Challenger believes their audience could accomplish anything if they had courage. With courage, they could see anything through. People could realize their dreams. Destinies could be fulfilled. Every problem can be solved with courage. If you use the Challenger frequency, your role is to elevate and deepen the amount of courage the listener is able to access for their own life. The room gains courage when you speak. People actually begin to grow in their faith and in their conviction that they can do hard things.

BAREFOOT ACROSS HOT COALS

The highest need the Challenger frequency meets is not simply courage. If you use this frequency, when you speak you are calling people to a mandate. You create a sense of calling people to their own destiny. When the frequency of the Challenger impacts an audience, they find themselves aspiring to more. They gain the courage to live out their calling. They begin to realize that they are capable of more. The powerful dynamic of the Challenger frequency is that Challengers do not just live their own courageous lives, they create environments where others elevate their intentions and aspirations.

Speakers like Tony Robbins embody the Challenger frequency. Tony has become known worldwide for doing more than motivating and inspiring people. He challenges them to change. One of his most iconic challenges at his events is to walk barefoot across hot coals. The image of people doing this became a symbol of someone stepping into their intention and calling. Tony's impact is about more than feeling courageous. He challenges others to embody the virtue of courage.

ONLY THE BEST WILL DO

Another icon of the Challenger frequency is Pep Guardiola, the manager of Manchester City Football Club in the Premier League. Watching the documentary *All or Nothing*, you see the Challenger frequency at work. Pep challenges his team relentlessly, even when they are outperforming their competitors. He always sees where they can improve and never settles for less than their maximum effort. Only the best will do.

Every frequency creates a culture. The Challenger creates a culture of activism and achievement. Those who thrive in this environment become the best versions of themselves.

If you encounter a culture filled with activists and achievers who always push the status quo and are never satisfied with mediocrity, you have stepped into a Challenger culture. If this frequency resonates with you, prepare to become your best self. When a Challenger's frequency aligns with your personal intention, you move toward becoming your most extraordinary self.

COMMANDER

THEMES
Authoritarian | Executor | Directive

FOLLOWERS
People listen because you carry
authority and are in charge.

POINT OF VIEW
"People need me to tell them
what to do and what must be done."

DRIVE
"I must move people to action!"

MARKER
Do others look to you to tell them what to do?

DYNAMIC
Activating

HIGH NEED
Direction

BASIC NEED
Trust

ICON
Bill Belichick

COLOR
Titanium

CULTURE CREATED
Conviction | Responsibility

www.thesevenfrequencies.com

Commander

He was quiet and unassuming for most of the journey. He seemed to be constantly observing and weighing every small detail as we traveled across the ocean.

It was only when the storm hit us unexpectedly that his presence became undeniable and essential.

We were seasoned sailors hardened by years working on ships with endless crews, but the intensity of the storm filled us all with fear for our lives.

The wind blew us side to side like a ragdoll.

All of our voices were swallowed up by the gale wind except for his. His voice cut the panic like a hot knife through butter. His commands were clear and decisive. There was no time to question or second-guess his orders. Without having to say so we all knew that our only chance for survival was to heed his commands with urgency and without question. His every word brought us both clarity and confidence.

In those moments, he was the master and commander. This is the power of the Commander frequency.

IN CONTROL AND IN CHARGE

The Commander frequency is the most utilitarian. This frequency is so powerful that it needs to be used at exactly the right times and in the right situations. The Commander is an authoritarian. Usually, people think of an authoritarian in a negative way, as someone who needs to be in control. We sometimes forget there are times in life when someone needs to be in charge.

There are moments you will be incredibly grateful when someone carries the frequency of the Commander. We need Commanders because they know exactly what needs to be done.

TRUST AND OBEY

People respond to the Commander frequency because it carries authority. Others intrinsically know Commanders need to lead. If Commander is your dominant frequency, you believe people need you to tell them what to do and what must be done.

Around 2003, I was invited to a dialogue with film directors Peter Weir, Peter Berg, and James Cameron. They were discussing their films, specifically the use of water in their directing. The focus was on Peter Weir's film *Master and Commander* starring Russell Crowe. It was set in the era of Napoleon, featuring a commander ordered to hunt down another ship through nearly impossible circumstances.

The story of *Master and Commander* reminds us that if you are at sea in the middle of a storm, you need someone who knows what to do. When you are in the middle of a battle zone, you want someone to be the authority leading you to a decisive victory. When in the middle of a crisis, you do not want a collaborator or someone committed to team-think.

I can think of several times in my life when the Commander frequency has been incredibly helpful.

My wife Kim and I had a dog named Thatcher. When Thatcher was a puppy, we brought her home and knew nothing about training dogs. We wanted a well-trained dog, so we hired a trainer. I thought the trainer would come and train our dog, but the trainer came to train us. The commands that mattered were not what the trainer told Thatcher, but what he told me and Kim.

Kim and I took two different approaches. Kim loved Thatcher and wanted to coddle her. I decided to follow the trainer's instructions to the letter. One day, Kim asked Thatcher to walk and Thatcher refused to move. When I commanded Thatcher to move, she walked.

Kim said, "You think you know everything about dog training, but you do not know anything." I replied, "No, honey, I do not know anything about dog training, which is why I'm doing exactly what the trainer told us."

Sometimes, you need to acknowledge you do not know what to do. Everything should not be a collaborative conversation. I did not need to give the dog trainer my recommendations. I just needed to listen and obey. The irony of this story is that my beautiful wife has, as her primary frequency, Commander. In fact, Thatcher was the only one in our home she did not command.

SPEAK WITH CONVICTION

About thirty years ago, Kim and I went white water rafting on the American River. It was one of the most intense seasons in the river's history. The rapids were at dangerous levels. We were on one of the last boats out before they shut the river down.

The guide told us it was his first solo run. Even though we were supposed to stay in the boat, everybody was jumping out and swimming in the water. The river, for at least the first hour, was nothing but calm. I think we were all convinced that they had overstated the potential dangers ahead.

When we hit the rapids, suddenly everyone jumped back in the boat. We did not know how to row in sequence. Everyone was doing their own thing. We saw a giant boulder up ahead and watched a raft hit it, flip, and throw everyone into the rapids. Then another boat did the same. Now we were paying attention.

Our guide, with his limited experience, needed to become the Commander. We turned to him, but we were doing more panicking than listening. Without realizing it, he had conditioned us to not listen to him. He had not held us accountable to the seemingly insignificant commands he was giving us. So now we were not predisposed to hear him in the middle of our crisis.

He tried to lead us. He tried to navigate us safely through the rapids. His voice was lost to us in the roar of the rapids. We rowed straight into the boulder, flipping and throwing us into the water. We weren't aligned with his frequency. What we needed was a Commander.

When the Commander frequency is critical, it must come from a trustworthy source. This is necessary so we can quickly align with a Commander's instruction. There are times you will need to access your Commander frequency. Stand in that authority, speak with conviction and clarity, and tell people what to do.

DO YOUR JOB

Some of our most compelling and controversial characters in film and television carry the Commander frequency. They span from Miranda Priestly in *The Devil Wears Prada* to Terence Fletcher, JK Simmons' character in *Whiplash*, to Joffrey Baratheon from *Game of Thrones*.

One of the powerful attributes of Commanders is that they build their authority through the basic need of trust. This is why the Commanders listed above are an editor in chief, a maestro, and a king. For a listener to give someone that level of authority in their life, there must be an equivalent level of trust. If people disengage when you try to access the Commander frequency, the necessary trust may not be there. Have you ever tried to tell someone else's kids what to do? How did it feel being ignored?

The Commander meets a high need in us for direction. People need to know what to do next in any aspect of their lives. Receiving that direction from someone is a critical part of effective communication.

The Commander frequency creates a culture where people follow with deep conviction because they have felt the leader's authority. One of sport's most iconic and successful Commanders is Bill Belichick, the former head coach of the New England Patriots. As an assistant coach and head coach, Belichick has competed in twelve Super Bowls and won eight. His team motto, 'Do your job,' is simple and powerful. It is not about inspiration or motivation. Belichick wants his players to know their role and do it well.

In the military, the Commander culture is prevalent. The film *Top Gun: Maverick* depicts this well. Iceman, an admiral in the US Navy, sends a note to his old friend Maverick asking him to come to his house. Maverick says something like, "It's not a good time," and Iceman responds simply: "It's not a request." In the military, commands are not requests. This culture of conviction is built on the confidence of rank, experience, and expertise.

SPEAK UP OR LINE UP

The Commander thinks in terms of action. The Commander frequency speaks in shorthand. Everything for them is logistical. They are moving objects from point A to point B. Commanders do not recommend, suggest, or imply. This frequency is completely directive.

The most positive effect of the Commander frequency on others is clarity and confidence. The most negative effect is compliance and control. When a communicator only uses a Commander frequency they can shut down any possibility for input and collaboration.

It is important to remember that Commanders speak in definitive language even when they are suggesting. Even when they are asking or requesting they may come across as if they are issuing an order. Commanders may be far more open to differing perspectives than their frequency conveys.

While it is not essential for a listener to respond to the Commander frequency with equal command, they must respond with equal conviction and confidence. Silence is interpreted as agreement. The Commander thinks, "If you have a better plan, speak up. If you don't, line up!"

CONFIDENCE AND CLARITY

Years ago, we shot a documentary with Karen Drijanski, chef and founder of Niddo restaurant in Mexico City. We enjoyed Niddo for years and got to know Karen. Outside her kitchen, she is warm and diplomatic. When she took me inside her kitchen for a tour, the first thing she said was, "Here, I am the commander." She spoke with a smile. "Here, I am in charge. Here, I speak and everyone does."

When you have the Commander frequency, you understand that in certain environments, you must lead with authority. A Michelin star restaurant. A war zone. Your child running into the street. Any place there is danger or alarm. You know what to do and you direct others to get it done.

HEALER

Counselor | Therapist | Developer

FOLLOWERS
People listen because you see them
and help them face their wounds.

POINT OF VIEW
"People need me to understand them
and help them understand themselves."

DRIVE
"I must create a safe space for people to heal."

MARKER
Do others look to you for empathy and compassion?

DYNAMIC
Relating

HIGH NEED
Wholeness

BASIC NEED
Acceptance

ICON
Oprah Winfrey

COLOR
Oakmoss

CULTURE CREATED
Nurturing | Therapeutic

www.thesevenfrequencies.com

Healer

H e knelt silently next to me without saying a word.

At first, I did not even know he was there. I had stumbled into this empty chapel somewhere in the woods near my home in North Carolina.

From my 15-year-old perspective my world had just come crashing down. My parents had just sat me down and told me they were getting a divorce.

Not being a particularly religious person, the likelihood that I would find myself kneeling at the altar of a small chapel in the middle of nowhere was pretty close to zero. Yet there I was. I am a bit embarrassed to admit I cried my eyes out until I basically ran out of tears.

I had no idea how to pray really, I was just there in silence trying to make sense of life. It would have normally felt pretty awkward that a stranger was kneeling so close to me without an invitation, but somehow his presence was comforting.

I noticed there were actually two of them- a father and his young son. They did not speak until I opened my eyes and looked in their direction. They looked at me with compassion and concern and simply *asked if there was anything they could do for me. An unexpected conversation ensued. I cannot remember exactly what the man said to me, all I can remember is how he made me feel.*

His words were like a healing salve to my soul. He spoke the language my soul needed that day and gave me the strength to face the pain that was still ahead. I have rarely experienced the power of the Healer frequency but this moment has never left me. I do not remember his name but I will never forget meeting him.

THE COUNSELOR

The Healer frequency is the counselor. This frequency connects to the broken parts of who we are. When you use the Healer frequency you make people feel seen. You help them face their wounds. This frequency embodies the universal truth that no matter who you are or what you have been through, all of us have wounds. Some wounds are obvious. Some wounds are more hidden. Healers have the ability to speak to the deepest wounds in our lives we think no one else can see.

If you live and communicate at the frequency of a Healer, you believe people need you to understand them and help them understand themselves. It is from the Healer frequency that we will most deeply transmit empathy.

MYSTICAL DYNAMICS

If you can connect with the frequency of the Healer, you can lead others through 10,000 sessions of therapy in one hour. You can help people process their pain and their struggles. The driving motivation of a Healer is to initiate the healing process in every person who listens. Carrying the frequency of the Healer is incredibly significant. I cannot overstate the value of the Healer in the world today.

Therapy is often used to help someone unwrap and identify their wounds. So many people who attend therapy find it one of the best experiences in their lives because they are able to talk about and process these wounds. One of the mystical dynamics of this frequency is that a Healer does not have to know a person or be in a dialogue with them to impact them. The Healer is somehow able to communicate in such a way that they can reach a stranger and connect to the deepest part of who they are. Their words go into the recesses of a listener's soul. Through communicating with this frequency, a Healer is able to begin to bring healing into people's lives.

YOU ARE NOT YOUR WOUNDS

The basic need the Healer speaks into is acceptance. They realize every human being first and foremost needs to feel accepted for who they are, no matter what they have been through.

This is the gift the Healer frequency communicates. Acceptance in your brokenness. Acceptance in your wounding. Acceptance in your imperfection. A recipient of the Healer frequency feels absolute acceptance for who they are or where they are.

When the frequency of the Healer begins to penetrate another person's soul, the Healer's acceptance opens the door for them to begin to accept themselves. So often, the healing process begins when you realize that you are not your wounds.

The Healer frequency elevates when a communicator begins to speak to our high need for wholeness. One of the peculiar things about individuals who operate at this level of frequency is that they see the entire world as broken. They believe it is necessary for every human being to face their brokenness. They want others to acknowledge their wounding and to begin the process required to move toward wholeness in their life.

PRESS THE WOUND

When you speak with the Healer frequency you can move people to an almost uncomfortable level of vulnerability. Someone may not have entered a room thinking about their wounds. They may be hiding their personal struggles or their brokenness. None of this matters. The moment you begin to speak, it all comes to the surface.

I am old enough to remember when Oprah first showed up on the scene. Oprah's daytime TV contrast was Phil Donahue. The Phil Donahue Show was built on controversy. It highlighted the worst in people and put it on display, and America loved to watch. The culture that was created out of that TV narrative was toxic and destructive to the human spirit.

Oprah showed up and all of a sudden, she went against all programming. She focused on what was right with people instead of what was wrong. Oprah did not highlight the worst in humanity to draw in more viewers. She began to create a conversation that communicated that all of us could be healed and become whole. We could be connected and move toward cooperation, collaboration, and community. Oprah uses her platform to bring healing, rather than simply press the wounds.

PERMISSION TO BE BROKEN

There are different people who use this powerful frequency to create the therapeutic counseling space that all of us need. I think of Mel Robbins, who is probably the most sought-after women's speaker in the US. Even though Mel often challenges people and calls them to more, so often what Mel's actually doing is sharing about her own anxiety and stress. Through her experience she helps people understand how she has developed different structures and tactics to move toward the best expression of herself. Mel gives us permission to be broken and then she gives us a pathway to be healed.

I see this same kind of dynamic with Simon Sinek, a brilliant author and speaker on organizational leadership. He communicates on multiple frequencies but his core frequency comes from his intention to speak to us in our brokenness. Not just the brokenness of an individual, but the brokenness of an organization. He breaks down companies and institutions and deals with their deep wounding without judgment.

That's one of the interesting things about Healers: they somehow are able to see us at our worst and still relate to us without judgment. They simply bring light to our brokenness and darkness so that we can be free of them, not so that we will feel judged by them.

NO INTIMACY WITHOUT VULNERABILITY

Jay Shetty was a Buddhist monk who is now a motivational speaker. When I listen to Jay, I feel that so much of his intention is to help you accept that it is okay to be broken and need help. He creates an environment that is therapeutic and nurturing, giving you just enough insight and counseling to move you forward in life.

I remember years ago when I was at TED Conference, a speaker came on stage that I had never heard of before. Her name was Brené Brown. Brown spoke about the importance of vulnerability and the power of removing shame. Most of us have never thought about removing shame as an act of courage. Yet Brown has sent out a frequency that has brought healing to hundreds of thousands, if not millions of people.

A SAFE SPACE FOR TRANSPARENCY

When you have the frequency of the Healer, you create a culture that is nurturing and therapeutic. A Healer culture will be designed for the person who needs the most time to heal. This results in a culture that waits for the last person before everyone can move forward. When a Healer is in leadership, the culture may become slow to change.

People will be drawn to your message. People will run to hear you speak. When you send out a frequency of healing, those who are broken and hurting and perhaps have been hopeless in their journey for wholeness will come and listen to your message.

The Healer sees people through their wounds. They are certain that everyone carries deep hurt within them that shapes who they are today. They often believe we are all defined by trauma, whether consciously or unconsciously. They have little patience for surface-level conversations and may begin to ask intrusive questions without invitation.

If the Healer frequency is activated without maturity, the Healer's input can feel invasive. Without wisdom they may see wounding in others that is not there and project their own wounding on those around them. Ironically, Healers can feel a loss of personal value if they are not surrounded by brokenness. This dynamic can cause a person receiving this frequency to either feel obligated to find a wound for the Healer to treat or become cautious of the Healer and hesitate to be fully transparent with them. The healthiest Healer environments are when Healers create a safe space for transparency and vulnerability.

The great challenge as a Healer is to always remember that you are emitting a frequency that moves people to the healing they need but you yourself are not the source of that healing. You are simply the voice of that healing.

THE MOST POWERFUL WEAPON

Historically, I think of Nelson Mandela, who embodied the Healer frequency and transformed the political landscape of an entire nation. Here you have a man imprisoned unjustly for the color of his skin, who lived in perhaps one of the worst modern expressions of racism on the planet, in the middle of apartheid within a society where the white Afrikaners had power, wealth, and position, while the black Africans lived in poverty, were powerless, and had no hope for the future.

As Mandela rose up to bring justice and freedom, he was imprisoned. Instead of becoming embittered, using that experience to harden himself and justify violence and revolution, Nelson Mandela sent out a frequency throughout the world that he would use his life to bring healing. If a nation ever needed therapy, healing, and an environment where peace could be nurtured, it was South Africa. Mandela believed that peace was his greatest weapon. Only peace could bring the justice that the nation desired and the freedom his people longed for.

Accessing the Healer frequency is perhaps the most powerful weapon in the world. When in concert with a complimentary frequency such as Commander, Challenger, or Seer, extraordinary things can happen.

PROFESSOR

THEMES
Teacher | Instructor | Mentor

FOLLOWERS
People listen because you help them
get the knowledge or skills they need.

POINT OF VIEW
"People need me to give them the
information they need to succeed."

DRIVE
"I must pass on the knowledge I have acquired!"

MARKER
Do others look to you to help them learn and understand?

DYNAMIC
Informing

HIGH NEED
Competency

BASIC NEED
Knowledge

ICON
Jordan Peterson

COLOR
Chestnut

CULTURE CREATED
Learner | Developer

www.thesevenfrequencies.com

Professor

The room was filled with entrepreneurs whose annual income was somewhere in the universe of $100 million. The event normally focused on strategies to create wealth and scale companies.

The room was filled with a clientele that focused much of their public persona on high-image management.

It was really important for most of the people in the room to be seen as more successful than they were, and they were already very successful. What I would have expected from the stage was a lecture on bitcoin or real estate development or franchising.

The speaker had expertise in every possible field that related to business. Everyone in the room knew he was a rare, strategic mind. If you needed someone to look at your problem objectively, he was your man.

So what came next was quite a surprise.

His lecture was mathematical and carried the weight of a legal argument. The facts were laid out like a meticulously constructed proof leaving little room for argument or disagreement.

For him, all truth traveled through the medium of data. He was all about the facts.

The curious thing is that his lecture was on happiness.

Yes, I said happiness.

Not wealth. Not power. Not success. Not fame. Not acquiring private planes or personal yachts.

Happiness.

This had become the focus of his research and he was certain he had cracked the code.

He shared his conclusions with equal parts objectivity and irrefutability. He had found the algorithm that would ensure the happiness that has been so elusive to most all of us.

We could not help but notice a certain disconnect. While he exuded confidence in his findings he did not emanate the same level of... well... happiness.

I am not saying he was not happy. I am saying that the frequency from which he spoke about happiness did not transmit his happiness to those of us who listened.

What we experienced was the objective transference of information.

What we experienced was the Professor.

For the Professor there is only one frequency that matters when transferring truth and that is the factual transference of data. The Professor believes it is only the truth that shall set you free.

PROFESSOR X

The frequency of the Professor is all about learning, teaching, and helping people gain the knowledge they need to succeed in whatever endeavor they are pursuing. People listen to the Professor because they help them acquire the knowledge and skills they need. If you carry the Professor frequency, you believe people need you to provide the necessary information for them to succeed in life. This frequency can apply to almost any domain, from politics to sports to science to business. Professors use their communication to transfer the information and competency that helps people learn and succeed. If learning is your highest value, then you and the Professor are on the same wavelength.

I grew up with graphic novels and one of my favorite narratives was the X-Men. I loved how an entire community was created through the leadership of one person, Professor X. Professor X was a unique superhero in that he was confined to a wheelchair. Professor X's superpower was his mind. He had the ability to communicate with anyone, anywhere, through his intellectual capacity. This personifies the frequency of the Professor. The Professor's superpower is their brain. Their strength lies in their thinking and data bank. The Professor wants to transmit the frequency of learning to elevate everyone who connects with them.

One of the films that shows the contrast that can exist within the Professor frequency is *Finding Forrester* starring Sean Connery as a reclusive writer. The film features three Professor frequencies at war. One is condescending, one is liberating, and one is emerging.

The genius of a young writer provokes two different responses from the two most influential men on his journey. The Professor frequency transmitted from Connery's character sought to elevate the intellectual capacity and journey of the young student. The character who played the young student's actual college professor had the same frequency but used it as a force of condescension. In both cases, we experience the power of the Professor frequency.

When operating at the highest level, the Professor frequency creates a voracious thirst for knowledge and learning.

A TERRIBLE THING TO WASTE

The basic need that the Professor addresses is knowledge. When I was growing up, there was a TV commercial that simply declared, "A mind is a terrible thing to waste." This would be the mantra of the Professor.

Someone who embodies the Professor frequency believes you have the capacity within you to become anything you desire and accomplish anything you want. The Professor thinks your greatness can be achieved through the accumulation of knowledge and skills.

The higher need the Professor speaks to is competency. To be an expert in anything, you must first gain the knowledge that will move you to the highest level of competency.

One well-known Professor is Dave Ramsey. I met Dave Ramsey about thirty years ago when he was just an individual, not the powerhouse he is today. Dave Ramsey has become a household name for financial responsibility. His mantra is, "Act your wage." He teaches people how to manage money and get out of debt. His mission in life is to give people the information they need to find financial success.

Years ago, my daughter Mariah discovered Dave Ramsey and he became her new hero. Mariah loves understanding everything she can about how to become financially successful and debt-free. She introduced me to Dave's work with Financial Peace and Financial Peace University. As a student at Financial Peace

University, Dave is your professor and he will teach you everything he knows so that you can become financially independent and free.

IDEAS WORTH SPREADING

Professors create cultures of learning and development. If you resonate with the frequency of the Professor, it is because you are driven to learn and lean into knowledge. You know learning is exactly what you need to get where you want to go. The culture shaped by a Professor is unique because it does not call for extreme change. The Professor welcomes incremental progress that leads to significant change.

I have attended TED Conference regularly and been part of the TED community for over 20 years. TED stands for Technology, Entertainment and Design. TED's curator Chris Anderson is an incessantly curious person and a voracious learner. It is no surprise that he leads a domain where the greatest minds come together to share their learning with the world. The theme of TED is "Ideas worth spreading."

Chris himself describes the most compelling part of a TED talk like this: "Your number one task as a speaker is to transfer into your listeners' minds an extraordinary gift - a strange and beautiful object that we call an idea. What is an idea, anyway? Well, you can think of it as a pattern of information that helps you understand and navigate the world."

Chris Anderson is a great example of a Professor because the stage is his, but he rarely chooses to stand there. He infrequently presents at TED. Chris introduces the conference, interviews different speakers, and will sometimes interject thoughts here and there. He is not trying to spread his own ideas. He wants to spread the ideas of others he believes everyone should hear. This is the essence of the Professor frequency.

Cornel West is another model of this frequency. West is an educator known for his work in social justice and cultural equity. He uses the Professor frequency to help people understand that information that can change their perspectives and perceptions of history and humanity.

Malcolm Gladwell is another distinct communicator who shares through the Professor frequency. Gladwell speaks primarily through writing. His many books include the bestsellers *The Tipping Point* and *Blink*. Gladwell makes his love of gathering and synthesizing information evident in his work.

If you love to learn and study, your core frequency may be the Professor. This frequency is about more than acquiring knowledge. It is about the love of transmitting what you have learned to others. When you enjoy taking the information you have gathered and turning it into insight for others, you know your frequency is that of the Professor.

SEE THE LIGHT COME ON

The Professor sees knowledge as the currency of life. Their right to be heard and to speak into your life is directly related to the expertise they have gained in their area of study. Their value is not for the primary acquisition of knowledge but in the secondary acquisition of knowledge. In other words, their knowledge is based on research, not necessarily on personal experience.

When the Professor frequency is textured through life experience it resonates with the listener and creates a deep transference of knowledge. The Professor, when operating at their highest level, lives to see 'the light come on.' This is when the Professor frequency has the power to bring enlightenment.

One of the most fascinating expressions of the Professor frequency is the story of Walter White in *Breaking Bad*. Even though the story takes a dark turn very quickly, everything Walter does is logical, mathematical and driven by data. What makes Walter both successful and eventually dangerous is that he keeps the emotion out of every decision. Long before the emergence of artificial intelligence, we have understood the danger of decision-making based only on data and absent of empathy. Walter's story begins with him being a very timid man choosing to enter a very dangerous world. His story ends with his infamous declaration, "I am danger."

LEADING GREATNESS

Phil Jackson could be considered a Professor in the sports world. As a basketball coach in the NBA, he won 11 championships. He coached prolific players like Michael Jordan with the Chicago Bulls and Kobe Bryant with the Los Angeles Lakers. He was not known for inspirational speeches as much as he was for bringing incredible insight into the game. Jackson understood his players and the game at a level few people ever do. He increased his players' knowledge and competency and created some of the best teams in the world. Phil Jackson's teams knew the Xs and Os and played with a deep understanding of their environment.

Jackson created a learner-developer culture where every single player got better.

The Professor frequency is powerful because it carries the belief that everyone can learn. What you might have thought was impossible to learn before suddenly seems within reach when you experience this frequency. Information leads to insight. Insight develops intuition. Intuition drives to action. The Professor frequency is not just about increasing what you know but transforming the way you live.

In its optimal expression, the frequency of the Professor uses information to change not just your mind but your life.

SEER

THEMES
Visionary | Futurist | Pioneer

FOLLOWERS
People listen because you paint a
compelling picture of a potential future.

POINT OF VIEW
"People need me to show them
the future that has yet to be created."

DRIVE
"I must open the eyes of the blind!"

MARKER
Do others look to you for a vision for their future?

DYNAMIC
Innovating

HIGH NEED
Innovation

BASIC NEED
Vision | Hope

ICON
Martin Luther King, Jr.

COLOR
Arctic

CULTURE CREATED
Futuristic | Risk-Taking

www.thesevenfrequencies.com

Seer

S he was a single mom raising three girls ages 11, 10, and 8. Her brother lived nearby and was the father figure the girls would not have had without him staying close. She often worked ten-hour shifts whenever the extra work was available.

Still, no matter how heavy her schedule, she and the girls had a nightly ritual they never missed. The girls' bedroom was cold and damp, with inadequate heat. They would bundle themselves up in blankets and sit close together on one bed to listen as their mom crafted them a story.

She would never read from a book even though reading was a family value. Bedtime was when she would tell of the adventures of three young girls who lived courageously pursuing the unknown, fueled by their insatiable curiosity.

Each night the characters took on new challenges and gained new skills as they stepped into a unique destiny.

What the girls did not know was that she was not just entertaining them; she was casting pictures of their potential futures. Each night she would project a vision of who they could become if they took on bravery, determination, and faith.

That each of them grew up to live extraordinary lives should be of no surprise. They were raised by a mom who every day would speak *to them in her Seer frequency. They pursued their dreams knowing no other way to live.*

LIVING IN THE FUTURE

The Seer communicates in a frequency that casts vision and expands imagination. The Seer is a futurist. Their communication opens up possibilities and opportunities for those who are listening. The Seer has the compelling ability to paint a picture of the future no one else can see until they speak. The Seer attracts people who are drawn to vision. Seers live with the internal drive to show others a future that has yet to be created.

Seers hardly pay attention to the past and barely live in the present. If you are a Seer, your frequency can be both intoxicating and maddening to others. You are always living in the future. Your focus lies in seeing where your organization or community can go. You dream of your future and the potential futures of those around you. The future can become so powerfully shaped within you that it becomes more real to you than the present.

When a person uses this frequency, those who are listening are pulled out of the past and present into a future-oriented mindset. This frequency is critical for the progress of humanity.

There will always be a need for vision. As we have been reminded even from ancient history: without a vision, the people perish. The more hopeless the time, the more desperate we need a voice that calls us to hope.

The Seer causes people to believe that their future can be different from their past. They know someone's present is not the end of their story. When you are a Seer, you are not simply creating a roadmap to the future. The Seer calls people into the future they alone can imagine.

VISION IS LIKE OXYGEN

The Seer's frequency speaks to our basic need for vision. You can access the Seer frequency if you are convinced that people will wither from the inside out if they lack vision. For the Seer, vision is like oxygen: essential, not supplemental.

When a person accesses the Seer frequency, they are not only casting vision. A Seer also calls people to the deeper need for innovation. The Seer knows that the future must be created through new, innovative approaches. All past practices of building or growing something are seen as out of touch or outdated. This is why the Seer frequency has a dual effect. A Seer creates a compelling picture of the future and also calls people to the processes that will make that future a reality.

TRANSFIXED AND TRANSFORMED

There are several indications that the Seer frequency resonates most deeply with you: You rarely find yourself living in the past. You are less naturally nostalgic even when someone reminisces. You leave little time for regret but instead quickly begin to reimagine the future. If you basically have no rearview mirror you carry the Seer frequency. The Seer frequency always calls us into the future.

If you want to experience a communication frequency that can greatly impact your life, find a Seer. The Seer frequency is rarer than many of the other frequencies and therefore garners large audiences. We should not be surprised when masses are moved by the compelling power of a Seer. The Seer frequency can be experienced both personally and corporately. When a Seer tells a story we are able to find ourselves within it.

George Lucas is a perfect example of this. He is the filmmaker who reinvented cinema with Star Wars. I remember the first time I watched Star Wars and felt transfixed and transformed by the vision of a future universe. Lucas did not just bring Star Wars to the world; he brought our imaginations a new way of seeing the future. Lucas translated his visionary frequency through film.

Virgil Abloh was a Seer. As the former creative director of Louis Vuitton, his ability to see and collaborate on visionary projects was unparalleled. It is not coincidental that he was introduced to the world by Kanye West, another Seer, whose frequency resonates with creatives who want to shape a different future.

Nancy Silverton is a Seer in the culinary world. She is the chef and entrepreneur who created La Brea Bakery and Mozza in Los Angeles. Her communication is through the artform of food.

Mary-Kate and Ashley Olsen are both Seers who evolved from child actresses into renowned fashion designers. The sisters communicate their visionary frequency through fashion, redefining the industry with their brand The Row.

THROUGH THE EYES OF FAITH

The Seer transmits vision that changes our view of what is

possible. We know we have been touched by the Seer frequency when we, too, see through the eyes of faith.

They may elevate our vision for the world, or lift us up to have a bigger vision for our lives. They may be calling us into their vision, or calling out of us our own vision. The Seer frequency repositions our hearts and minds towards the future.

Often the vision they share is both exhilarating and terrifying. Depending on our receptivity and resonance with the vision, we can experience the Seer frequency as either a fresh breath of air or an unwanted gale wind throwing everything off course. While the Seer transmits a frequency fueled by the magnetic pull of a compelling future, they also invite us to believe that this potential future can be created together.

The Seers call us to leave the past so that we can create the future.

EXPANDING IMAGINATION

Wherever there is a Seer in leadership, their frequency creates a culture of innovation and risk-taking. Whether it is their family, their community, or their organization, the Seer always calls those around them into the new and unknown. You cannot create the future without risk, and the Seer destabilizes the present to make way for what could be. The power of the Seer is that they erase the boundaries of limitations, expanding imagination and causing you to contemplate the impossible as possible.

One of my favorite quotes comes from the Book of Isaiah. It reads, "Put away the former things; do not dwell in the past. Behold, I am doing a new thing. Now it springs up; will you not be aware of it?" The Seer sees the new thing. With a Seer, the future begins as a dream and becomes a reality.

One of history's most powerful Seers was Martin Luther King, Jr., whose 'I Have a Dream' speech captivated a nation and propelled civil rights forward:

"...Even though we face the difficulties of today and tomorrow, I still have a dream. It is a dream deeply rooted in the American dream. I have a dream that one day this nation will rise up and live out the true meaning of its creed: We hold these truths to be self-evident, that all men are created equal...

I have a dream that one day on the red hills of Georgia, the sons of former slaves and the sons of former slave owners will be able to sit down together at the table of brotherhood...

I have a dream that my four little children will one day live in a nation where they will not be judged by the color of their skin but by the content of their character. I have a dream today...

And when this happens, and when we allow freedom ring, when we let it ring from every village and every hamlet, from every state and every city, we will be able to speed up that day when all of God's children, Black men and white men, Jews and Gentiles, Protestants and Catholics, will be able to join hands and sing in the words of the old Negro spiritual: Free at last. Free at last. Thank God almighty, we are free at last."

The power of the Seer is to inspire others to see the invisible and together create what was once only imagined.

MAVEN

THEMES
Iconoclast | Outlier | Heretic

FOLLOWERS
People listen because the mystery is unsolved.

POINT OF VIEW
"People need to explore the unknown."

DRIVE
"I must liberate us from our false view of reality."

MARKER
Do others look to you for the unexpected?

DYNAMIC
Innovating

HIGH NEED
Paradigm Shift

BASIC NEED
Curiosity

ICON
Albert Einstein

COLOR
Medallion

CULTURE CREATED
Pioneering | Imaginative

www.thesevenfrequencies.com

Maven

My wife Kim asked me to come to Lilongwe, Malawi to celebrate the culmination of seven years of her work with tribal leaders to bring education and development to this region of Africa.

She had secured a meeting with the president of Malawi as well as leading members of the government.

The primary reason we were making the journey across the world was that after nearly a decade and more than $1 million invested, her team finally completed building a model education center for more than 1,600 students spanning from 1st to 8th grade.

Over 1,000 people from the neighboring tribes would be coming together for the campus' dedication ceremony, led by over twenty tribal chiefs and dignitaries.

Kim generously made sure every representative from Mosaic - our church in Los Angeles - had a suit to wear for the ceremony. She was aware that political dignitaries and the traveling chiefs would all be wearing suits to reflect the importance of the day and the significance of the ceremony.

Kim knew that it would be important to the tribal chiefs that we dress in a way that had become appropriate for diplomatic events. Even though I understood this, I could not shake the thought that these tribal chiefs wore suits because of the influence of Western missionaries decades before.

Kim herself is the most grounded and down-to-earth person you could ever meet. She would never go to any culture and impose her personal value system on them. At the same time, she is huge on respect and honoring established protocol.

That morning, Kim and I had a fairly intense conversation about how I would dress for the ceremony. She was pretty insistent that I wear the suit she brought me. I understood her point and it was a point well-made, but something inside me did not allow me to conform or cooperate.

For me, it wasn't about wearing a suit. It was about the worldview and paradigm I would be advancing. I kept thinking, "What is the story I must tell?"

It was so clear to me that I needed to destroy and create.

It was impossible for me to explain what I saw in any way that made sense to her.

Instead of the suit, I wore a pair of repurposed pants, a t-shirt, and a multicolored hoodie made of old Kantha Ralli South Indian quilts.

If I did not mention it, I was the event's keynote speaker.

The event was held on a soccer field that was more of a dust bowl than a pitch due to the absence of grass.

After the festivities and the speeches from all the dignitaries, it was my turn. I slowly walked into the center of the field.

As I positioned myself facing the tribal chiefs who were seated in the places of honor, I suddenly knew what I needed to do.

I sat down in the middle of the field. To them, I was a visiting chief. It should have been beneath me to sit on the ground at their *feet. I sat there in silence for a moment, allowing the imagery to sink in and the awkwardness to permeate the moment.*

I then began to explain to them that if I had come to them representing the United States government, I would be wearing a suit. If I were there representing a major NGO or humanitarian organization, I would also be wearing a suit.

I was dressed as a simple man and sitting on the ground because I was there representing the person of Jesus. I was sitting at their feet because we were there to serve them. I was sitting in the dust because nothing was beneath Him, so nothing was beneath us.

If I were there to represent God, there was only one posture I could take, and it must be the posture of humility. I knew I needed to help them see God from a radically different vantage point.

The message that I felt entrusted to share with them required I be willing to communicate at a frequency that they had perhaps not yet encountered. I knew it would be jarring but communication is more than words. We are the carriers of our own frequencies.

We could not remain in the story they had been told about those who followed Jesus. The old story had to be destroyed so a new story could be written.

Kim would tell you that I do not make simple things easy. All of our marriage she has wanted me to fit in and find acceptance. I understand why my beliefs and life choices would be seen as defiant and nonconformist. It's not that I don't want to belong. I just don't see the world, or life, or reality, the same way that others do.

The Maven frequency is not about making incremental shifts within the commonly held reality.

The Maven frees your mind to see reality from an entirely new vantage point.

ALIEN PLANET

Mavens see the world as an alien planet and humans as a peculiar species. While the world searches for answers, the Maven searches the world for questions. Mavens seem trapped in the maze of self-reflection and inception. Reality is a suggestion. They are drawn to mystery and uncertainty. It might go without saying that the Maven is the most misunderstood frequency.

As a Maven, you may unintentionally communicate in a frequency others cannot understand. If your core frequency is the Maven, you may experience confusion with how difficult it is to relate to others. A Maven may spend their life learning to communicate and connect to the many but are mostly embraced by only the few. A Maven's frequency finds the people who love innovation, revel in exploration, and are themselves outliers.

To the majority, the Maven frequency brings distress. The Maven is innately heretical, treating the sacred as open to questioning and inquiry. Their violation of orthodoxy is rarely conscious or deliberate.

REDEFINING THE GAME

The Maven is often not an expert but a student with endless curiosity. They are seen as connoisseurs of new ideas. They can become the one everyone looks to for expertise in a particular domain, topic, or area. Ironically, they are the same ones challenging the pillars of belief in each of these domains. In any arena - sports, mathematics, space, culinary arts, politics - the Maven is the one redefining the game.

When the Maven realized the forward pass was not illegal in American football, they changed the game forever. The Maven changed the Olympic high jump from the classic Western Roll to the Fosbury Flop. The Maven bent the laws of science and proposed that mass and energy are the same. When the Maven is an artist, reality is reimagined on a canvas and Cubism is created.

When a Maven surrenders to nihilism they become the evangelists of a dystopian future. Mavens create expressions depicting this future in films like *Inception*, *The Matrix*, and the classic *Blade Runner*.

The Maven sees Earth as merely a starting point and spends their life preparing humanity to occupy Mars and inhabit outer space. Elon Musk is perhaps the most iconic Maven of our time. Whenever I hear Musk speak, I resonate with his frequency. From creating SpaceX with the ambition to move humanity to Mars, to founding Tesla and revolutionizing the auto industry with electric vehicles, Musk is an outlier. He not only dreams but invests billions to turn those dreams into reality.

For the outside observer, many of Musk's financial choices seem irrational and even irresponsible. What most of us have a hard time understanding is he simply does not see reality the same as the masses. I do not think it would be unfair to say that in the mix of his genius there is at least a touch of madness. For one of the wealthiest men in the world, he does not seem to care about money at all. After all, what is another mansion here on Earth when you are trying to colonize the galaxy?

PARADIGM SHIFT

The basic need met by the frequency of the Maven is curiosity. The Maven is needed most when we are trapped within self-limiting frameworks. The Maven helps people see reality through an entirely new lens.

Aside from provoking curiosity, the Maven is driven by the high need to bring about a paradigm shift. The Maven knows that if they can change how you see something they can change what you see. A particular vantage point can change the way you see everything. The true Maven sees reality from a completely different paradigm than the majority of the population.

The Maven lives in paradox. They find it perplexing that we humans hold so tightly to our orthodoxies and certainties. The comfort certainty brings to others eludes them. They often do not know what they know. They know what they do not know.

What they do see clearly is the difference between a truth and a belief. We hold beliefs. Truths hold us. Therefore, we can search for truth with open hands. Mavens are not careless with truth; they simply do not see truth as fragile.

They do not think outside the box; they have never seen the box. They question everything. They wonder how others have found such certainty and even envy it. They live in a loneliness of the mind and yet their minds are crowded with an endless cacophony of voices. In many ways they are strangers to the real world, and they feel most at home in their inner world.

Leonardo da Vinci imagined the future in ways that seemed impossible in his time. He envisioned the submarine before the technology to create one existed and imagined the helicopter generations before flight technology was developed. Da Vinci did not simply improve on what existed. His imagination lived in the impossible. Everything he imagined was an introduction to an alternate reality.

NOTHING IS SACRED

The Maven frequency causes tears in the fabric of the universe. When this frequency is used without wisdom, a person can be experienced as reckless. When the Maven operates at the highest level of the frequency, they remove the scales from our eyes to see where we were once blind.

This is why the Maven frequency can be so misunderstood. In their search for truth, they will be seen as a destroyer of truth. The only thing sacred to them is the purity of the pursuit. This can be destabilizing to those who are impacted by their message. The Maven is often unaware they have discarded things sacred to their listeners.

I remember years ago I was invited on a TV show hosted by Brian Houston, the founder of Hillsong Church. Just before we went on air, he began to share with me a somewhat cryptic explanation of why I had always made him nervous. To put it simply, I just did not fit into any of his boxes.

As unlikely as it may seem, and believe me, no one was more surprised than me, I not only became a person of faith, but I became a pastor. The Maven frequency is my most natural frequency, and this has made me an unlikely candidate for starting a church and being a pastor.

I founded a community of faith called Mosaic in 1993. My work at Mosaic was seen as outside of the acceptable lines of orthodoxy. In case you are unfamiliar, churches tend to be profoundly rooted in the past and tradition. From the beginning, I knew that Mosaic was a social experiment with a spiritual intention. We described ourselves as the church's R&D department.

One of our central tenets was the integration of creativity and spirituality, a thought that was considered heretical thirty years ago. My view of the future also made me an outlier. The moment I proposed that the future was dynamic and was created by human choice, it added another layer of my heresy. Even our name was seen as suspect since it did not say "Church." Not to mention, we first started meeting in a nightclub once owned by Prince.

Every facet of who we were and how we expressed ourselves as a community violated what many thought was permissible in the church. We did not consider ourselves a contemporary church or a modern church. We were determined to be the epicenter of the future of humanity.

Mosaic became a place of refuge for creators, innovators, artists, pioneers, and outliers all over the world. At the same time, Mosaic became the focus of derision among those who were the gatekeepers of orthodox Christianity.

This is why both Brian and I were surprised he invited me to join him. Right before we walked on stage, I turned to him and said, "Remember, today's heresy is tomorrow's orthodoxy." He looked particularly distressed and simply responded, "I hope not."

I just had to laugh.

MAVEN MASTERCLASS

We live in an extraordinary time in human history. Previously, few had access to the frequency of Mavens. Elite environments provided access to the greatest thinkers, mathematicians, philosophers, chess players, artists, composers, and painters. Universities were developed to facilitate the exchange of ideas but rarely from those who thought outside the box. Today, we have unprecedented access to Mavens in any field we want to explore.

We have Masterclasses in every conceivable domain. The first Masterclass I watched was Steph Curry teaching how to shoot a three-point shot. As the greatest shooter ever, his genius is what draws us in. Steph has reinvented the game of basketball, and it will never be the same again. Similarly, I love diving into Masterclasses from world-renowned directors and writers whose uniqueness sets them apart rather than simply their expertise. We are often more compelled by the person who is most original than simply the one who is technically the best.

THE CRAZY ONES

If your natural frequency is that of a Maven, you are rare. The gift of this moment in history is the availability of contrarian thinking in every conceivable field. You can learn faster and grow more quickly by accessing the frequency of the best in the world. Though Mavens are rarely exceptional public speakers, their unique approach towards seeing the world can inspire and elevate the listener's longing to find their own voice. More often than not Mavens will need a translator to speak to the masses. They are, after all, the crazy ones.

I will never forget the night I sat watching television and 'the' commercial came on the screen. I had never seen anything like it. It was like a siren calling us into the deep blue ocean. It was exhilarating.

In 1997, Apple launched a revolutionary campaign called 'Think Different.' Below is the text from the ad that captivated me. It feels as if it was written directly to emerging Mavens and anyone who would aspire to be one.

Here's to the crazy ones. The misfits. The rebels. The troublemakers. The round pegs in the square holes.

The ones who see things differently. They're not fond of rules and they have no respect for the status quo. You can quote them, disagree with them, glorify or vilify them.

About the only thing you can't do is ignore them. Because they change things. They invent. They imagine. They heal. They explore. They create. They inspire. They push the human race forward.

Maybe they have to be crazy.

How else can you stare at an empty canvas and see a work of art? Or sit in silence and hear a song that's never been written? Or gaze at a red planet and see a laboratory on wheels?

We make tools for these kinds of people.

While some see them as the crazy ones, we see genius. Because the people who are crazy enough to think they can change the world, are the ones who do.

Finding Your Voice

The starting point to navigate the seven frequencies is to identify your core or primary frequency. Your core frequency is
the singular frequency that is most natural to you when you
communicate. It is your default mode. It is the way you communicate when you are not even thinking about communicating. It is the way you communicate at home. It is the way you
communicate with the people closest to you.

IDENTIFYING YOUR CORE FREQUENCY

There are people you interact with every day of your life. I do not
mean your casual acquaintances, even though how we communicate with them is still significant even if brief. It is the people
that matter to you most that give us our primary context for
communication. If you are married, it is your spouse. If you
are a parent, it is your children. It is also your close friends and
colleagues that you work with on an ongoing basis. They are the
ones that know you from your primary frequency.

One way to discover your core frequency is to ask the people in your life. Sit down with them, walk them through the

seven different frequencies and ask them which one they identify as your core frequency.

Do not say, "Hey, I'm a Healer. What do you think?" or, "I'm
a Motivator. Do you agree with me?"

Here are a few prompts that might help you:

"When I speak into your life…"

1. Do you feel motivated? (Motivator)
2. Do you feel challenged? (Challenger)
3. Do you feel told what to do? (Commander)
4. Do you feel understood? (Healer)
5. Do you learn something you didn't know? (Professor)
6. Do you feel inspired with a bigger vision? (Seer)
7. Do you feel confused and wonder if I've lost my mind?
    (Maven)

You could even ask, "Rate these from one to seven. The one
you hear me as the most, and the one you hear me as the least."
They may not have a clear sense of the middle, but they will
probably have a very clear sense of what frequency you use all the
time and what frequency you never use.

There's another way to identify your primary frequency: what
frequencies are you most drawn to? What frequencies inspire you?
What frequencies match your wavelength? When you hear someone speaking and think, "Wow, they are on my wavelength," what
does that wavelength communicate? If you listen to a Professor
teaching and passing on information and go, "Wow, I really get
them. They really get me," that is a great way of knowing the

Professor is likely your core frequency. If you hear a Seer cast vision and it is right in your sweet spot, your core frequency may be Seer. You get them, you understand them. The way you hear is often the way you speak.

Of course, you could invest in yourself, put in the work, take our online assessment and dive deeper into understanding not only your frequency but the frequency of those who matter most in your life. You can take the assessment today at www.thesevenfrequencies.com.

DEFAULT MODE

You may have a core frequency that is not creating the outcome you desire. No matter how much you try to clarify yourself, you never seem to be able to communicate effectively with certain people. You try to operate in a different frequency, but you always find yourself going back to your default mode. If you naturally speak from the Challenger frequency, your friends may keep telling you that you need to be more of an encourager, but you always move back to challenging. Or you may have people in your life who need you to be a Healer, but your core frequency is the Commander. You always find yourself having to apologize because your communication comes across as too directive and authoritarian when others want you to be more of a therapist and counselor.

DYNAMICS

Frequencies create action. We speak not only to be understood but to create. Each frequency has a dynamic effect on the listener.

The Challenger and Commander are both activating frequencies. These frequencies move people through calling them to action.

The Motivator and Healer are both relating frequencies. These frequencies move people through investing in a personal relationship with them.

The Professor is an informing frequency. This frequency moves people through sharing information with them.

The Maven and Seer are both innovating frequencies. These frequencies move people through revealing a new future to them.

Whether your voice most naturally moves people through activating, relating, informing or innovating, the end goal of all communication is transference. The miracle of human communication is that it connects us to one another and allows us to move together into a shared future.

OUTCOMES

Step number one to identify your core frequency is to seek input as to how other people hear you. Step number two is to pay attention to how you best hear others. There is one more step to help you find your core frequency.

When you communicate, which approach usually helps you achieve the best outcomes? You will discover that this is the frequency with which you most naturally and effectively engage others. It is your core frequency that almost comes as muscle memory. It does not require you to think operationally about how to communicate or how to find the perfect language. This is what comes inherently out of you. When you want to express yourself authentically, your core frequency is what gives you the best odds of success.

Remember, whatever your core frequency is, it is the most natural one for you. There is no right or wrong starting point. There is simply your authentic voice, and the best communicators always speak from their authentic selves.

The Dark Side of Us

There is a series I find fascinating called *Succession*. It is a drama about a billionaire who pits his four children against each other to compete for who will succeed him as CEO of their family media conglomerate.

People who study the seven frequencies will often ask me to tell them the frequency of a person or a fictional character. One day a friend asked me, "What are the frequencies of the characters in Succession?"

I froze. Nothing came to mind.

For a moment I was panicked. What if this system was broken? What if I had missed something crucial in how people communicate?

The characters in Succession are not good people. They act in their own best interest to the detriment of everyone else. None of them seemed to fit any of the seven frequencies.

And then I realized I was approaching the answer from the wrong direction.

The characters do carry the seven frequencies, but only in their shadows.

Their communication was devoid of goodness and light. Instead, it was dark. Empty. Ultimately tragic.

Which makes this a good place to introduce the dark side of each frequency.

The distortion of a frequency creates a shadow. All of us are capable of having a dark side. It should not surprise us that if our soul is filled with jealousy, envy, bitterness, hatred, that our internal state would affect the transmission of our frequency. Our frequency both expresses us and exposes us.

GOING TO THE DARK SIDE

The shadow of your frequency appears when your frequency is inverted from focusing on others to focusing on yourself. Shadows reshape how you communicate. Where a natural frequency will seek to serve others, a shadow frequency serves only you.

Operating in the shadow of your frequency limits the incredible impact your authentic frequency can have. This is why it is so important to understand that your communication frequency is deeply connected to the health of who you are as a human being. The shadow is not in the frequency, the shadow is in us. The frequency is an expression of our internal state of being. You cannot separate the essence of your communication from the essence of who you are.

SHADOW #1: THE MOTIVATOR
AS PERFORMER

A Motivator operating in their frequency inspires and encourages other people. A healthy Motivator creates environments that are positive, optimistic and transformative. When the frequency of a Motivator becomes corrupted the speaker shifts into a Performer. If you are a Motivator who operates in your shadow, you place more importance on how your audience feels about you than how you feel about your audience. The Performer is driven by the need to be accepted or affirmed. The Performer can transform authentic communication into a superficial exercise. At their worst, the Performer becomes a con man. This shadow harms the integrity of the Motivator's message. A Motivator naturally receives energy from encouraging others. If you operate too long as a Performer, you will begin to feel incredibly exhausted always being on.

A Motivator guards against their shadow when they make applause secondary and choose to focus on transforming environments and elevating others. If you are a Motivator, use your frequency to lift people, elevate energy, and build self-belief in others.

SHADOW #2: THE CHALLENGER AS MANIPULATOR

The Challenger frequency is always about calling the best out of people. When you carry the Challenger frequency you believe in people so much that you know they are always capable of more. When the frequency of a Challenger is corrupted the speaker shifts into a Manipulator. A Challenger's communication calls people to aspire toward their highest self. If you are a Manipulator, you call people to what you need them to do or be or accomplish. This is a very subtle but powerful frequency shift.

A Challenger's natural influence makes it important that the frequency is focused on calling people to their best selves and their best life. A Challenger wants to inspire results. A Manipulator wants to coerce results. If you operate in the Manipulator shadow, you get people to act on what they do not want to do for your benefit. When you operate in the Challenger frequency, you get people to do what they deeply want to do but lack the courage to pursue.

The toll of constantly operating from the shadow of the Challenger is that those who desire to be close to you do not feel safe enough to trust you with their vulnerability, weakness or wounding. The way to redirect the shadow back to the power of the Challenger is to work on behalf of others, helping them achieve the goals they have set.

SHADOW #3: THE COMMANDER AS DICTATOR

Commander is a powerful frequency that carries authority and inherent trust. A Commander uses their frequency to move and arrange people. When a Commander operates in their frequency with integrity, they direct others to the highest good they can accomplish together. When the Commander frequency is corrupted the speaker shifts into a Dictator. The Dictator seeks to eliminate individual will and personal choice. The Dictator is fueled by the desire to fulfill their own wants and needs.

Dictators are offended by questions and often refuse to offer explanation for their decision-making. A Commander is focused on executing to achieve a mutually desired outcome. A Dictator is focused on forcing others to submit to their will. A Commander is focused on the good of the whole. A Dictator is focused on the good of the self.

When you continuously operate from the Dictator frequency you begin to mistake compliance for loyalty. You begin to see people as tools to achieve your desired outcomes. When the Commander lives in their shadow the toll of the harshness of this frequency results in isolation and eliminates the opportunity for genuine human connection. The best way for a Commander to come out of their shadow is to place themselves in accountable relationships and to seek to treat both peers and subordinates with the highest level of respect.

SHADOW #4: THE HEALER AS CIPHER

The Healer frequency is most effective when a communicator brings healing and wholeness to others. There is a powerful therapeutic narrative in the wavelength of the Healer. When the frequency of a Healer is corrupted the speaker shifts into a Cipher. The Healer creates an environment of empathy. The Cipher creates an environment of co-dependency. The Healer releases empathy. The Cipher consumes empathy. When a Healer shifts into their shadow they confuse the power of their message with their own inherent value as a healer. The Cipher is convinced people need them directly and personally to find wholeness. A Healer seeks to heal others. A Cipher seeks to heal themself. One of the most dangerous things is to use your platform and relationships to heal your own wounds. When operating from the shadow of the Healer, you use the wounding of others as your own source of therapy. The shadow consumes the pain of others rather than bringing the healing and wholeness they need.

The toll of the Cipher is that while they paint a picture of having an infinite capacity to heal others, they are quite often drowning in their own pain and brokenness. When you are the Cipher you cannot ask for help. To admit your need is to disqualify yourself in your own mind. To move out of the shadow of the Healer you must be willing to be honest about your own pain, brokenness and wounding. The only path from the Cipher to the Healer is that of authenticity and transparency.

You can recognize the Cipher when they see themselves as the singular source for your healing. If you become dependent on them for your healing, you have entered the gravitational pull of the Cipher.

SHADOW #5: THE PROFESSOR AS DIMINISHER

The Professor frequency communicates the knowledge and wisdom others need to grow and develop. A Professor focuses on the development and enlightenment of others. When the frequency of a Professor is corrupted the speaker shifts into a Diminisher. A Diminisher is convinced no one understands a subject at their level of expertise. A Professor's tone informs. A Diminisher's tone condescends. A Professor believes their role is to expand the mind of the student. A Diminisher believes that what a student needs is to come face to face with their ignorance. Where a Professor encourages someone to pursue learning even if they fail along the way, a Diminisher punishes a learner for every misstep in their study. A Professor uses information to enlighten. A Diminisher uses information to demean.

When a Professor lives in their shadow, they lose their capacity to keep learning. Their shadow creates in them a fear of being discovered lacking in any area of expertise. The very attribute that makes the Professor frequency invaluable becomes corrupted by the need to protect the image of knowing rather than the hunger to know. To move out of the Diminisher shadow begins with three transformative words: I don't know.

SHADOW #6: THE SEER AS PERFECTIONIST

The Seer frequency casts vision and calls people to the future. The Seer frequency sets people free and moves them forward. When the frequency of a Seer is corrupted the speaker shifts into a Perfectionist. When the Seer is fixated on an ideal future, they can become paralyzed by the need for perfection. The Perfectionist rejects any outcome that is not the pure reflection of their vision. They will stop the creative process because the execution is imperfect. The Perfectionist holds others to a standard of achievement only they can visualize.

A Seer trapped in their shadow is held hostage by their vision. Waiting for perfection leads to paralysis. The Perfectionist shadow creates an oppressive force inside the speaker where nothing will ever be good enough. When you use the Seer frequency, the future will never look exactly as you imagine. While your vision may be perfect, the journey is filled with imperfection. Involving others in the creative process means the future evolves to be more complex and more beautiful.

To reclaim the Seer frequency and move out of its shadow, your vision has to be about people, not simply outcomes. The Perfectionist sees vision as a static image of the future. To leave this shadow, you must once again engage vision as dynamic and adaptable to the gifts and talents of the people around you.

SHADOW #7: THE MAVEN AS NIHILIST

The Maven frequency destroys commonly held views of reality. A Maven confronts a listener's viewpoint without regard to the sacredness of their beliefs. Mavens do not try to elevate the thinking of others; they try to liberate their minds from the constructs unconsciously holding them captive. When the Maven is corrupted their frequency turns them into a Nihilist.

The shadow of the Maven rejects the orthodoxy of the world around them without offering a better and more holistic alternative. Everything is off. No one knows what is right or true or good. When operating as a Nihilist you know why everything is wrong, but you have no idea what is right. The consequence for those who are impacted by the Nihilist's frequency is that they lose hope in creating a better world. The Nihilist sees the flaws in our present way of thinking without leading us to a better way. The Nihilist frequency sees only a dystopian future.

The great danger for a Maven who is living in their shadow is that it translates into despair. The genius of the Maven becomes only a madness. For the Maven to reclaim their frequency and break free from the shadow that can too often haunt them, they must recognize that simply because they cannot see the way forward does not mean there is not one. For the Maven everything is seismic and almost never incremental. Yet to escape their shadow, the Maven must learn to celebrate the beauty and wonder of the world around them.

APPLYING THE SHADOWS

In the example of Succession, the patriarch Logan Roy is a Commander turned Dictator. He never asks; he commands. Everyone around him is only a guest in his universe. Unlike a Manipulator, Logan Roy does not try to hide his coercion of others. He is in charge. He uses people at will. He considers all thoughts that do not align with his as rebellious and quickly squashes them.

Logan's most likely successor is his son Kendall Roy. Kendall is a Seer turned Perfectionist. He can see a future where he is CEO but he cannot get there. He consistently betrays his ideals and morals in an attempt to create a future where his father loves him. He has the vision necessary to make the company succeed but is imprisoned by his dysfunction.

Logan's daughter Siobhan is a Challenger turned Manipulator. She constantly attempts to orchestrate her family members to benefit her personal ambitions.

The youngest son Roman is a Motivator turned Performer. He is not naturally suited to the family business and takes on the role of the clown to avoid personal responsibility and his father's anger and disapproval.

The final son is Connor. Connor is technically the eldest child but intentionally removed himself from the CEO competition. He is a Healer turned Cipher whose childhood was devoid of affection. He devotes all his time and wealth to winning the love of his ambivalent girlfriend who is actually a call girl paid to care about him.

Siobhan's husband is Tom Wambsgans and he embodies the Professor turned Diminisher. He is an executive at the company but has low confidence in his ability to do his job well. In his own mind, he has the expertise to lead the company, but he has never done anything that would validate his self-belief. He takes an unpolished young man named Greg under his wing only for the opportunity to belittle and demean someone with even less power than him.

The outlier character is Greg. He is the Maven turned Nihilist. You're not sure if Greg is completely incompetent or the only genius in the room. Greg's character seems completely focused on surviving. Perhaps the most disturbing line ever uttered from his lips was when Tom asked Greg if he wanted to make a deal with the devil and join Tom's betrayal of the family. Greg simply responded, "What am I going to do with a soul anyway?"

One of the most difficult questions I have personally had to struggle to answer is why we as human beings are so drawn to the shadow frequencies. It is inescapable that the shadow frequencies have great power and have a disproportionate amount of influence in the public domain. It would be an understatement to say it is disconcerting how powerful the shadow frequencies are in the present culture. If you are purely utilitarian, you would conclude that accessing your shadow would have a greater impact than using your authentic frequency. Of course, this conclusion is short-sighted and does not measure the destructive power of the shadow both to ourselves and to others.

I have identified at least two dominant reasons why we are drawn to the shadows. The first is our wounding. If when you were a child, you longed for the love and affection of someone who related to you as a Manipulator or a Dictator or a Cipher, you would continue in your adulthood to seek the affirmation of the very same shadows that wounded you throughout your development. If you identify yourself as a person drawn to shadow frequencies, the first place I would look is within yourself - your own trauma and pain that has not yet been resolved.

The second dominant reason that we are drawn to the shadows is that we, too, are living in them. Or should I say hiding in them. If you are a Performer, you are comfortable with Performers. If you are a Manipulator, you are comfortable with Manipulators. But it goes deeper than that. We are drawn to the shadow frequencies when we want the outcome they have achieved without regard to the means with which we attain them. In other words, you see a Manipulator accumulate great wealth and your desire for wealth overrides your desire to live an authentic life. You take on the shadow in hopes of gaining a similar outcome. But in the words of Jesus, "For what profit is it to a man if he gains the whole world, and loses his own soul?"

The Internal Architecture of Communication

In this chapter, we will create a map of the seven frequencies using the internal architecture of our mind.

Understanding your natural design is crucial. Once you identify your primary frequency you can then integrate other frequencies that will best serve the moment you are in. We will walk through the seven frequencies and their interrelationships. To illustrate this process, I will share my own communication journey.

INHERENT TO WHO YOU ARE

When I consider my childhood, the first frequency I can identify is the Maven. When I first started looking at the seven frequencies, I thought maybe the Maven frequency was something you develop over time or something that comes in adulthood. I realized that if this frequency is inherent to who you are, you have been speaking on this frequency all your life.

Part of the way you know that the Maven frequency is your dominant frequency is that even when you were young, you were thinking and talking about things in an unexpected way. You might have been discounted or written off as being crazy. People may have been continuously surprised by your perspective or vantage point.

This early frequency in my life did not work to my benefit. Sometimes your primary frequency may actually work against you. If your child has the Maven frequency, it is not going to be that helpful to them when they are in elementary school. Through the continual development of the frequency, the Maven becomes an incredible gift and advantage.

PUBLIC SPEAKING

When I began speaking in a public environment, the first frequency I took on was that of a Seer. I began immediately talking about the future, showing a different picture of where humanity could go. From the seminal part of my own communication journey, people would talk to me about being a visionary. It seemed that whenever I spoke, people had a bigger vision. They began to expand their imagination. They began to see new possibilities for themselves and the world around them.

At the same time, I began to cultivate the Challenger frequency. Imagine listening to a 23-year-old Challenger who saw it as their mission to shake things up and call out everyone in the room. It did not go well.

The Maven, the Seer, and the Challenger became the core cluster of my communication style. I moved between them very readily and easily. Over time I began to realize that sometimes one was more important.

I would enter certain environments or certain crowds and see they needed a little bit of vision and a lot more challenge. I could sense that in one environment they would not accept me as a Maven, and to use that frequency would only discredit me, not give me more credibility. Part of my communication education was learning how to navigate those frequencies effectively as I moved from place to place.

THE FURTHEST FREQUENCIES

The frequency that was furthest from me was the Commander. This authoritarian frequency was so unnatural for me that many times people would ask, "Would you just please tell us what to do?" When our kids were growing up, they would say, "Dad, I do not want advice. I just want you to tell me what to do." I think it is a pretty rare thing for your kids to come to you and say, "Just tell us what to do." Because I almost never operated as a Commander, that deficit created a value for the frequency in their life.

The Professor frequency is also rare for me. My early perspective was that if the information was available, you could get it for yourself. I realize now why the Professor is so essential and important. Without the Professor, I often did not give people the ABCs of an idea. I would jump right to XYZ. This left people unable to actualize and apply what I was teaching them.

The Motivator was my fifth frequency. Early on in my leadership journey, people on my team would say, "Hey, could you tell me what I'm doing right?" or, "Could you just encourage us?" or, "Could you just let us know what we've done that you really appreciate?" Sometimes the direct ask was, "Could you just affirm us?"

I would tell everyone, "You are doing a great job."

Eventually, they would come back to me and say, "Hey, that is too general. 'You are doing a great job' doesn't feel genuine. If you really think we are doing a great job, could you tell us specifically what we are doing that is a great job?"

This revealed to me that I am not a person who naturally needs a lot of external motivation or encouragement. This led me to assume other people did not need encouragement either.

OPERATIONAL FREQUENCIES

If my top cluster is Maven, Seer and Challenger, and my bottom cluster is Commander, Professor, and Motivator, between those lives the Healer.

The Healer frequency was not in my top cluster, but it quickly became one of my most operational frequencies. As a speaker, I discovered that when I shared my own pain and struggles it created an incredible connection with the audience that the Maven, Seer or Challenger could not achieve. In my best moments, I would literally pause in the middle of my message or presentation and access the Healer frequency. When I operate in the Healer, my entire message is elevated to a different level.

IN REAL TIME

I want to illustrate how all of the frequencies move together when you communicate.

I recently spoke at The Summit of Greatness, an event sponsored by my friend Lewis Howes.

As I prepared, I actively chose not to begin with the Challenger frequency since I was new to the audience. Often, an audience will not receive the Commander or Challenger frequency without first establishing and building trust.

I knew that the moment I stepped on the platform I would naturally move into my Maven and Seer frequency, but I deeply felt that people in the room needed the Healer. I wanted to make sure I did not miss the Healer moment, so I did something I rarely do. I began my entire message absolutely focused on communicating from the frequency of a Healer.

Starting with my own wounds, I connected to the wounds of the room. My intention was solely to connect to their need for healing and wholeness. It was transformative. Suddenly the entire room was with me, and we had just met.

From there I moved into the Maven frequency, which was very unexpected. It is a mental jump from brokenness to a radical shift in thinking. This combination of frequencies opened up the entire room to a new conversation.

ACCESSING YOUR WEAK SPOT

So many times, I have to remind myself that the Commander frequency is the frequency furthest from me. In my speaking notes I may purposefully write down, "This is where you need to tell people what to do."

There have been times I thought I was so authoritarian that I was the pinnacle of the Commander, issuing commands left and right. Later on, my team would inform me, "Yeah, you never did that."

When the frequency is far from you, just stepping into it a little bit can feel like overkill to you. The reality is that when a frequency is less intrinsic to who you are, you almost have to overcompensate and step into it at a deeper level until you find a middle ground that is comfortable for you.

For example, if you start as a Commander and decide to move into the Healer frequency, it is probably going to take all the energy you have. If you are naturally a Motivator, it may be incredibly difficult for you to become a Challenger. You are so intrinsically designed to communicate the frequency of an encourager that it is hard for you to confront people.

EXPANDING YOUR TOOLBOX

For each frequency, you have complementary frequencies and counterprogramming frequencies. However the internal architecture of your brain is designed, you will move most naturally from your primary frequency to your primary's most similar frequency. For example, if your primary frequency is the Motivator, you may move most easily into Healer. You shift from giving energy to extending wholeness. From Healer, the closest frequency on the spectrum is the Professor. You shift from extending wholeness to sharing knowledge. You expand on one frequency, then move to the next one, and then add the next one. There are frequency compatibilities that seem to cluster together more than others. You may also naturally move between two frequencies throughout your day. Before you know it, all seven frequencies are in your toolbox, and you can access whatever frequency you need to connect.

Expanding and Refining
Your Voice

S ound is a fascinating thing. I have a confession to make: I have a really high level of noise sensitivity. I have a hard time being in a room where there is an immense amount of noise all happening at the same time. It feels chaotic.

If you try to operate in a communication frequency that is not your natural frequency, at first it is not going to be a frequency. It is going to be noise. It will take time and dedication to expand your access to each frequency. This is why it is so important to seek to understand who you are and then build out from your core frequency to the frequencies that are most naturally accessible to you.

One of the things I have learned to do over the years is to give young communicators an unexpected prompt right before they walk on stage. Usually, the prompt is around a frequency they do not naturally activate but will give them incredible momentum. I know if they can activate this frequency, it will interact with their natural frequency and create a much more powerful presentation.

Life will require you to use certain frequencies at specific times. Together we will unpack how to activate the frequency you need.

ACTIVATING THE MOTIVATOR

The key to the frequency of the Motivator is the word affirmation. What Motivators do is create a space and environment where people feel incredible affirmation. The best way to activate the Motivator frequency is to train your brain to work from optimism and to fill your soul with hope.

The best Motivators know how to celebrate incremental progress. One of the great challenges when you are not a natural Motivator is that you do not even know *what* to celebrate because you cannot see the incremental progress a person or team has made. If you want to ignite the Motivator frequency, look for the small changes that you can affirm. Look for the small victories that you can celebrate and begin to talk about them.

ACTIVATING THE CHALLENGER

I remember many times with one of our speakers, I would go up to him right before he walked on stage and say, "You need to go up there and pick a fight. What are you mad about? You can pick your subject: you can be angry about injustice, you can be angry about poverty, you can be angry about despair, you can be angry about hopelessness, you can be angry that people do not have meaning in their life. Just pick something before you walk on the platform, get angry, and pick a fight."

I am not saying that anger is the optimal emotional fuel for communication, but it can be a great catalyst when it is focused in the right direction. To access the Challenger, it can help to get angry about the things that are wrong in the world. Call them out! Then pick a fight to make them better. Call them up!

ACTIVATING THE COMMANDER

There are times people simply need you to tell them what to do. You are not telling them what to do because you need to be in control. You are not telling them what to do because you need to be in charge. You are not telling them what to do because you are an authoritarian dictator. You are telling them what to do because your training, expertise, or experience positions you to know exactly what they *should* do so they can actualize their highest selves and experience their highest success.

You need to see the moment where you move into the Commander frequency as the moment where you are doing the most good for people. You are helping them save so much time that they could have spent stumbling around, trying to figure things out. They would have been reaching in the dark and you know where the light is. So, tell them what to do. Do not suggest. Do not create some kind of metaphor. Just be straightforward, be concrete, be linear. Be a Commander and watch people thrive.

ACTIVATING THE HEALER

I have known many talented speakers and polished communicators who had a natural skill for oratory. Their difficulty was they never gave any of themselves when they spoke. As a listener, you never felt you knew them better after you heard them.

You experienced a great presentation or a great talk but they walked off the stage a stranger, just like they walked onto the stage. If you are going to become a Healer, you need to be honest about your own pain.

I remember a time I spoke into a really gifted communicator. I said, "All right, the next level is waiting for you, but you have a ceiling, and the ceiling is going to be about your ability to become vulnerable."

I continued with, "If you choose to become vulnerable, you will become a world-class communicator. No one can make you vulnerable. I'm not telling you that you *should* become more vulnerable. What I'm saying is that if you aspire to be a world-class communicator, you are going to have to choose to move to this uncomfortable space of vulnerability."

He laughed awkwardly and said, "Yeah, I don't think I can do that." It became his communication ceiling. When you activate the frequency of a Healer, you have to move to a level of honesty that can make you feel naked. It can be uncomfortable to be honest about your own pain, shortcomings, and struggles, but this level of vulnerability is the foundation of the Healer frequency.

ACTIVATING THE PROFESSOR

If you are going to activate the Professor frequency, you have to have ideas worth spreading and believe that information can change a person's life. The best way to activate the Professor frequency is to ask yourself this question: what truth or insight has actually changed me? The best way to activate the Professor frequency is to learn so that you may teach. Develop a voracious appetite for learning and then pass on what you have learned as fast as possible.

Remember, you do not really learn something until you apply it. Knowledge is not simply about information; it is about integration. The way that you ignite the Professor frequency is to teach what has actually changed you. You do not have to know everything about math, science, literature, or philosophy. Put into words what has changed your life and teach others.

ACTIVATING THE SEER

Though the Seer frequency is more rare than most of the other frequencies, all of us need to absorb vision for our lives. Even when it is not our dominant frequency, humans are designed for vision and thrive best when we live with a compelling vision for our lives. If you are not a natural Seer, you need to realize that it does not matter if your vision is self-generated or gained in community. All that matters is that it is truly yours. To activate your Seer frequency, get around other Seers.

If the Seer frequency is one of the most distant frequencies from your primary frequency, you may always feel a little bit out of place when trying to use the Seer to communicate.

Here is the really good news: when a natural Seer uses their frequency, they may be painting a picture a thousand years in the future, a hundred years in the future, twenty years in the future, or even ten years in the future.

Most people do not have a vision of a future so far ahead in time. Most people actually need a vision for this week, this month, this quarter, or this year. The way to activate the Seer frequency is to not try to be a person who can see fifty years into the future when it is not natural for you. What you want to do is get a clear picture of the short-term future in front of you.

Cast a vision for what future you are going to create right now. You will find yourself communicating at the Seer frequency and inspiring others to begin to create that future together.

ACTIVATING THE MAVEN

I want to remind you that the Maven is a rare frequency. If the Maven frequency is not intrinsically in your core design, it is going to be very challenging to access.

First of all, you need to know it will take you time to access your inner Maven. If it is not your natural frequency, you are going to have to make a lifetime commitment to remaining endlessly curious and open. So, here's how you become a Maven: find your obsession and push yourself to the edges. Find a topic, area, or arena that you are passionate about, obsessed about, and own that arena. Develop expertise. Know it better than anyone else. Make no assumptions. Question everything. Then watch how you will begin to have breakthrough ideas. Remember, a Maven frequency is not about knowing more than everyone else. The Maven is about seeing things in a way that the world has never seen. The only way you are ever going to see something from this vantage point is to become obsessive about that topic, subject, or area of expertise.

Subtle Differences, Significant Synergies

When you are first interacting with the seven frequencies, some of them may seem very different while some can seem more similar. All the frequencies are part of a universe. Like sound waves, some sounds blend together better, while other sounds create more dissonance. It is the same way with communication frequencies. You may be immediately comfortable using one frequency while another frequency feels almost dissonant to yours. Yet there will be times you will be required to combine those very two frequencies and it will feel like the most unusual emotional, psychological cocktail. The dissonance, though, can create the most dynamic communication experience imaginable.

If you are operating from a Commander frequency and a Healer frequency at the same time, you are doing the seemingly impossible. This may be more like playing jazz compared to using two other frequencies that are more aligned such as the Maven and Seer, or Motivator and Healer. Let us take a moment and unwrap some of the nuanced differences between the frequencies.

THE MAVEN, THE SEER & THE PROFESSOR

You might see some similarities between the Maven, the Professor and the Seer. A person could have these three in their cluster and they can work in an incredibly harmonious way. The nuanced differences are that a Seer is a visionary who sees a different picture of the future and calls people to create that future. A Professor is an instructor who takes existing knowledge and translates it to his or her students. A Maven is presenting ideas that have never been imagined or thought. So, while a Professor is working from what can be known, a Maven is actually communicating from what is unknown.

Even though they may seem similar in their level of expertise, it is a dramatically different expertise. The Maven speaks at a frequency that very few people will connect to because what they communicate will seem as if it is impossible, or that they are out of their mind. By contrast, a Professor is incredibly grounded. A Professor draws from facts. They are working from data and historical context. A Professor is incredibly credible because they build their credibility on what can be known, and now they are passing that knowledge on to you.

A Seer is a visionary who elevates the possibilities of what can happen or what can be done. A visionary is not necessarily a Professor or a Maven. They are not radicalizing a new idea that has never been conceptualized, and they may not actually be working from the knowledge of what can be known and passing it on to another. The Seer is more of an activist, creating a risk-taking, innovative environment. A Maven can have an idea and never act on it. A Seer is always moving forward toward a new vision of the future. A Professor may not be an activist and may not be a visionary, but they are convinced that the solution to every problem can be found in the knowledge already available to us.

THE COMMANDER, THE CHALLENGER & THE MOTIVATOR

There is an interesting relationship between the Commander, the Challenger, and the Motivator. The Challenger and Motivator can seem very similar until you realize that the Motivator is driven to create an environment of encouragement and affirmation. The Challenger, on the other hand, may not be interested in affirming or encouraging but in persuading and calling you to a higher level of execution. The Motivator is more concerned with how you feel about yourself, while a Challenger is more concerned about you becoming your future self.

You might think, "Wait a minute. That sounds like the Commander." But the Commander and the Challenger are very different.

The Commander is not interested in persuading you. They are not interested in challenging you. They are simply interested in telling you what to do, when it needs to be done, and how it needs to be done. It is a directive, logistical frequency that says, "You need to trust me. I know what needs to be done and you need to do it."

A Challenger may not actually tell you what to do. They are more focused on the amount of effort you bring than a specific action for you to take. A Challenger may say, "You must bring your best." A Commander, on the other hand, says, "To be your best, you need to do this..."

THE HEALER, THE COMMANDER & THE CHALLENGER

The three least likely frequencies to work together would seem to be the Healer, the Commander and the Challenger. Yet, what I have found is that even though these are unlikely pairings, they actually work in concert very well. Some of the most effective communicators I know are able to emit a Commander and Healer frequency at the very same time.

Although I have not given him the assessment, I would assess that one of my great friends, Ed Mylett, is this brilliant combination of frequencies. Ed is a global entrepreneur who is ranked as the #1 speaker in the world. He transmits a powerful confidence where you are more than willing to do what he tells you, while at the same time transferring the frequency of a Healer, creating a safe space to bring your wounding. I would go as far as to say that when you hear him in his optimal communication flow, he also adds the Challenger frequency. It is very rare to be called to great things, to be told what to do, and to feel your inner world being healed at the same time.

DISTINCT TRAJECTORIES

The seven frequencies each communicate to different people, are embraced by different people, and are each effective based on the uniqueness of the circumstance. For instance, when there is nothing but chaos and confusion people become most open to the Commander frequency. A person who embraces a Professor frequency because they believe in the power of the classroom and learning may be completely resistant to a Maven frequency because they think the Maven is speaking in the realm of impossibilities and living in an ethereal, fanciful world that will never exist.

One of the great challenges as you engage with the different frequencies is that even though they may seem subtly nuanced in the beginning, the frequencies each have very distinct trajectories. The ways they impact the listener and translate into life change are incredibly different.

Your frequency creates a momentum, and that momentum will lead the person who embraces your message to a completely different application. That is the strength of your frequency. The best communicators access the frequencies the same way an orchestra conductor elevates the different instruments to create the perfect symphony.

Unleash the Power of Your Frequency

I have lived in Los Angeles for nearly thirty-five years and have been involved in the Hollywood community and entertainment culture for decades. One of the well-known adages of the industry is this infamous quote: "It took me a long time to discover that the key thing in acting is honesty. Once you know how to fake that, you've got it made."

Communication at your frequency's highest resonance is a combination of two dynamics: authenticity and empathy. When a speaker has a lack of empathy, they do not fool the audience, but they can fool themselves. The speaker may believe they are connecting with the audience, but the audience knows the speaker is not one of them. Empathy makes you one with the listener.

There may be nothing more dangerous than a person who has learned how to inauthentically express authenticity. I remember years ago my son Aaron began communicating to large audiences for the first time. My recurring advice was always, "I just want you to be your authentic self."

There was so much pressure on him to be polished and perfect. He knew how to capture an audience, but I wanted him to give himself room to be raw and vulnerable. I knew he had deep empathy, but it would not be experienced as powerfully by the audience if he chose to be guarded.

I remember one day he responded to my appeal to simply "be authentic" by asking me a question.

"Dad," he said, "what if my authentic self is inauthentic?" That may be the most honest response anyone has ever given me. We both looked at each other and laughed.

A PROCESS, NOT A PLACE

We tend to think of authenticity as all-or-nothing. We are either authentic or inauthentic. We leave no room for any degrees of variance on a spectrum when it comes to this trait. Yet the reality is that part of the human dilemma is that our most authentic self is a process, not a place. We do not arrive at authenticity; we fight for it. I choose the word authenticity with some degree of hesitation. Frankly, depending on the definition you accept, I am not always for a person being their authentic self.

One definition of authenticity is 'representing one's true nature.' If what you really want is to steal my car, I absolutely do not want you to be your authentic self. I would like for you to be inauthentic and not steal my car. If your authentic self is that you are greedy and selfish, I would not want to encourage you to be your most authentic self. If who you are most authentically is an angry person who is desperate for vengeance or retaliation, I would rather you not act on the real you. If authenticity is simply expressing who you really are, then inviting you to become your most authentic self can be a dangerous invitation.

I am using the word authenticity with a very distinct bias. When something is authentic, it is not false but genuine to its original intent. When something is authentic, it is trustworthy, reliable, and original. When something is authentic, it is true. Authentic communication results in life change.

The impact of even an incredibly skilled communicator will be damaged if they are inauthentic. To achieve maximum effectiveness, you must match your authenticity with your frequency. The type of frequency is irrelevant. Authenticity grounds and expands every frequency in the soul of the listener.

SHARE A SOUL

Empathy is not simply about understanding someone; it is about resonating with them. Empathy creates an experience with another person where you have a shared soul. There is no separation between you. You feel what they feel. You see what they see. You understand the world from their perspective.

Empathy comes out of your essence. It is like a muscle in the soul. Empathy is not a skill; it is a value. Empathy begins with listening. It elevates with active listening, and then travels far past listening to deep understanding. This is where transference works in the opposite direction. Empathy is not about transferring what is inside of you to another person, but transferring what is inside of them into you.

You are at the beginning of empathy when you can look another human being in the eyes and say, 'I understand you.' You will know true empathy emanates from you when the person can respond, "You see me."

I am convinced every healthy human being has empathy. For some the muscle is smaller than for others and it needs to be strengthened. Developing this level of empathy might be most difficult for someone with a Commander or Professor frequency. It may come most naturally to the Healer and Motivator frequencies.

If you are a person for whom empathy is not natural, begin with the person you love the most in the world. If you do not know how to embody how others feel, you will always be limited in your communication. Without empathy, you are walking through the human experience blind.

OPTIMAL COMMUNICATION

Optimal communication happens when there is synergy with both authenticity and empathy. Authenticity is the baseline. This is formed in the *character* of the person carrying the message. Empathy is the variable. This is formed in the *connection* of the speaker to their listener. Authenticity is how much of yourself you bring, and empathy is how much of the listener you bring. Authenticity is about your deep connection to yourself; empathy is about your deep connection to others.

Frequency is the outcome. The level and strength of a speaker's frequency is determined by their authenticity and empathy.

COMPLEX CREATURES

When our frequency is expressed without empathy, it diminishes in its force of impact. When our frequency is expressed without authenticity, it produces a shadow. Our shadows must not be seen as absolutes. We may be sincere in our intent to help others and yet still find ourselves speaking from our shadow and not our light. This can happen for many reasons.

It can be as simple as our fear of being known. It can be the result of the success we have achieved while still carrying a persona. It can be that we have the courage to be vulnerable in some areas of our life but not others. Humans are complex creatures, and how we express ourselves is simply not black and white.

You might even find yourself traveling from your shadow to your light in one singular conversation or presentation. We are all susceptible to image management and performing. We are also all vulnerable to feeling inadequate and unsafe and can choose to become self-protective. We can be tempted to take shortcuts to success and use our shadows to our advantage. Unfortunately, all of us can learn the power that can be accessed through our shadows to achieve our desired outcomes.

From my perspective, communication that is used for any destructive means is inauthentic and corrupted. For instance, I would not consider lying communication. Lying does not create communion but separation and isolation. The goal of communication is connection. Lying wants to control, not communicate. Control is the opposite of connection. Dishonesty is the enemy of communication. Deception is the enemy of communication. Manipulation is the enemy of communication.

DISCOVER YOUR AUTHENTIC SELF

The film director Steven Spielberg was asked to name a favorite movie that he did not direct. The film he chose was *Lawrence of Arabia*, an extraordinary epic filmed in 1962. Spielberg loved *Lawrence of Arabia* because the main character, T.E. Lawrence, was an accomplished, commanding officer who struggled to know himself. Despite its massive cinematic background and budget, the film is an intimate portrayal of Lawrence's angst. Lawrence lived with an extraordinary sense of loneliness because he only knew himself through the perceptions of others. The film is a brilliant reminder that perhaps our greatest accomplishment in life is to know our authentic selves.

You must decide to discover your authentic self. As long as you are held captive by the opinions of others, your identity will be dominantly shaped by what other people say and think about you. To know yourself, you must come to a place where what other people say is irrelevant to your identity. This is a lifelong journey. I am not saying that it is easy.

When you decide to pursue authenticity, you are freed from a life of image management. You do not have to live worried or concerned or shaped by other people's judgment.

I should warn you. When you come to know yourself, you may not like yourself at first. Everyone assumes that when you discover who you are that you will like who you find. You may come face to face with the person you have been running from all of your life. The journey towards authenticity begins the moment you are willing to do the hard work to become the best version of you.

Growth can be avoided when we are satisfied pretending we are someone else. Eventually it catches up with us. It is simply too exhausting trying to be who we are not. Sometimes we do this because we are trapped in self-loathing. We can like who people say we are better than who we know ourselves to be.

To find your authentic voice is to accept the fact that when you see yourself, you may not like yourself fully. In the face of this, you have to learn how to love yourself. You can love yourself and still not like everything about you. What is important is that you are willing to change as a human being.

You don't have to be perfect to be a great communicator, but you do have to be authentic. When you embrace your humanity with all of its imperfections, that is when you find your authentic voice.

The synergy between authenticity and empathy is undeniable. When you move toward your authentic self you grow in natural empathy. Your frequency will always reveal your level of authenticity and empathy. The deeper your authenticity and empathy, the more powerful your frequency. If you aspire to be a great communicator then first be a true human. Find your voice. Then speak life into the world.

Essence

There is an ancient text that has shaped three of the world's most dominant religions: Judaism, Christianity, and Islam. It also contains the formative worldview from which the Enlightenment and the age of modern science have emerged.

The five books known as the Torah begin with the book of Genesis. The first recorded words from Genesis chapter one are attributed to God himself.

The creative act from which the entire universe comes into existence is initiated through the power of the spoken word.

It begins with one declaration:
"Let there be light."

Whether you read this account of the beginning of all things as history or mythology, the intention of this story remains true all the same.

Creation begins when it is spoken into reality.

The entire universe is the manifestation of what God spoke into existence.

Since the beginning of the scientific revolution, these words seemed more myth than reality.

The possibility that light came before matter seems more poetic than probable.

Yet now we know the entire universe is the materialization of energy, of light.

I do not take lightly that the same scriptures tell us that we are created in the image of God.

We, too, have the power of speaking reality into existence.

The secret of the power of manifestation is that our words do not so much change the world around us as change the universe within us.

Do not let this realization lead you to underestimate the power you have to change the world around you. It is the universe that is created within you that has the force of power to change the world around you and even create a future only you can imagine.

Our words are power. Words shape who we are.

Communication is not simply about transmission; it is about transference.

Communication at the deepest level is not the sharing of ideas but the sharing of ourselves.

Communication is how we breathe life into each other.

Communication is the transference of essence from one soul to another.

Communication is a spiritual act.

The words we speak carry a power for which we must take responsibility. What you say to yourself will shape who you become.

What you say to others will shape the impact you make on the world around you.

Our words create universes within the souls of those around us. When you speak, you are creating.

The power of life and death is held within your lips, guided by your tongue, and given life by your breath.

Each of us is either declaring that there be light or surrendering to an ominous darkness.

We are both bound together and entangled by our words. When we feel unheard, we feel alone. Maybe that is why we are so desperate to be heard by as many people as possible. It is a curious thing that we would find more affirmation by having thousands of followers who do not know us than to have one person who actually knows us well.

You can only find your voice when you know yourself. You can only be truly known when you are understood. You cannot love another human being if you do not long to understand them.

Without communication, there is no connection. Without connection, we drift in the abyss of loneliness. There is a language that is deeper than words, but it can only be known when our frequencies are in tune.

With my simple understanding of reality, I have changed my mind on what it means to be human. When I was young, I thought of us as the composition of flesh and blood and bone.

Later in my life, I began to see us as a complex composition of water and earth and wind and fire. Recently, I have come to see us through the template of particles and waves. If our particles entangle us, then our waves expand us.

I once thought our skin had to touch for us to have a profound and intimate connection. Now, I know that my soul travels as far as my waves do.

Your sound waves do not simply send out your thoughts and ideas. Your sound waves are an extension of you.

I have two arms. They are not simply an extension of me, they are who I am. My arms are as alive as I am. That would be true for my two legs as well as my heart and my brain. We never think of the parts of who we are as not being alive. They are alive because we are alive. We are alive because they are alive. If my heart dies, I die.

Clearly there are parts of us that are more essential for life. I can live without a hand, but I cannot live without my heart. We tend to think of our words as a nonessential extension of who we are. Something less a part of who we are than our hair follicles.

Your words are more intimately connected to your essence than your heart or your brain.

They are connected to your soul. However you identify your core essence, that is the place from which your words come. Your words are as alive as you are.

At least in the poetic sense, as long as your words speak you are still alive. If your voice never goes silent, you will never be conquered by death.

Ironically, in the first chapter in the Book of John, Jesus is described as the Word. He was in his essence the physical manifestation of the thoughts and words of God.

It would be no small tragedy to live your life speaking in a frequency others cannot hear. If we do not learn how to listen, we will never know how to be heard. Understanding your frequency is not a self-indulgent process. It is essential for human connection.

All of us are on a journey to be understood.

Perhaps an even greater journey would be to harness the ability to understand others.

The beautiful thing is you can have this confidence: there are people in the world who need to hear the message you have been entrusted with, in the frequency you speak from most naturally. I am convinced all of us have unlimited capacity to master the full spectrum of human communication and connection.

The seven frequencies carry within them the beautiful spectrum and brilliant colors of human communication. This is the hidden language of human connection.

The gift we can all give each other is to learn to listen to the frequencies from which people speak with understanding and without judgment.

The goal of great communication is connection. Great communicators create a transference. When you find your voice, you find your power. When you harness your frequency, you unlock the creative power that resides within you. Ultimately, my hope is that as we unlock the power of the seven frequencies, we unleash the power of speaking life into one another.

There are some people who have perfect pitch. They can hear a note and know exactly what it is and even reflect it back. Imagine having perfect pitch when it comes to hearing the frequency of those who are desperately trying to connect with you.

When you can hear someone's frequency, you have given them an incredibly beautiful and intimate gift. When you hear their frequency, that person will feel fully heard and fully seen.

Communication at its most human level is not simply the transference of ideas but of hope and love.

As I said when we started this conversation, I do believe words are magic. Yet they are so much more. They are life.

ACKNOWLEDGEMENTS

I would like to express my deepest gratitude to everyone who played a role in bringing *The Seven Frequencies of Communication* to life.

First, I want to thank my favorite Commander - my wife, Kim. You have steered us confidently through waters rough and calm.

To my family, Aaron, Mariah, Jake and Juno Boogie, I want to live on your wavelengths. I study the frequencies of communication so that I can best tell you how much I love and appreciate you.

To my Arena Publishing team, Aaron C. McManus (our CEO), Austin St. John, Alisah Duran, and Brooke Figueroa, thank you for your commitment to elevate and equip others to break every ceiling and live the life they were created to live.

To my team at Mosaic, thank you for your tireless work to send the frequency of hope around the world to those who need to hear it most.

Tess Roy, thank you for returning to us and joining our creative team for the cover artwork. You create through the frequency of excellence and beauty.

Thank you to Xavier Cornejo, for your friendship, guidance and expertise, and to Anchor Distributors, for helping us get this book out in the world.

ABOUT THE AUTHOR

Erwin Raphael McManus is a mind, life, and cultural architect and an award-winning author and artist. His books have sold over one million copies and have been translated into more than a dozen languages. As a world-renowned communicator, McManus has spoken to millions of people in over 100 countries on six continents in stadiums of up to one-hundred thousand people. His creative genius has resulted in consulting work with organizations spanning from the NFL to the Pentagon.

McManus has spent the last thirty years advising and coaching CEOs, professional athletes, celebrities, billion-dollar companies, universities, and world leaders, and is passionate about helping people destroy their internal limitations and unlock their personal genius.

A native of El Salvador, McManus is recognized internationally for being the founder and lead pastor of Mosaic, a spiritual movement that has inspired millions worldwide. He and his wife, Kim, also lead humanitarian work across the globe. McManus coaches leaders, entrepreneurs, and communicators worldwide through McManus Mastermind and co-founded The Arena, a global community of learners and leaders focused on the three pillars of communication, leadership, and character, with his son, Aaron C. McManus.

To discover more from Erwin McManus, including his groundbreaking work on The Seven Frequencies of Communication, visit www.erwinmcmanus.com.

THE 7 THINGS YOU CAN DO IF
YOU ENJOYED THIS BOOK:

1. If you haven't yet, unlock your core frequency by taking The Seven Frequencies assessment, available at www.thesevenfrequencies.com

2. Share a review of *The Seven Frequencies of Communication* and tag me at @erwinmcmanus.

3. Join The Arena, a community of like-minded people seeking to understand the art of communication and elevate their leadership. Find more information at www.thearenasummit.com.

4. Join us at the Arena Conference. Find more information at www.thearenasummit.com/conference.

5. Listen to the *Mind Shift* podcast, co-hosted with Aaron C. McManus at www.erwinmcmanus.com/podcasts.

6. Explore the Mosaic podcast for messages that will inspire and transform your inner world at www.mosaic.org/podcast.

7. Check out my other books at www.erwinmcmanus.com/books.